Slim and Healthy
MEDITERRANEAN
Cooking

Slim and Healthy
MEDITERRANEAN
Cooking

JUDITH WILLS

PHOTOGRAPHY BY DEBBIE PATTERSON

CONRAN OCTOPUS

FOR MY FAMILY

Throughout the book, recipes are for four people unless
otherwise stated.

The Publishers would like to thank Pepita Aris and the following
shops and organizations for the use of fabrics, glass, tableware
and other accessories used in the photographs:

The Conran Shop, 81 Fulham Road, London SW3 6RD
The Perfect Glass Shop, 5 Park Walk, London SW10
Designers Guild, 277 Kings Road, London SW3
Souleiado, French Provincial Fabrics, 171 Fulham Road, London SW3

Editorial Direction: Lewis Esson Publishing
Art Direction: Mary Evans
Design: Peter Butler
Photography and Styling: Debbie Patterson
Illustrations: David Downton
Food Styling: Janey Suthering
Editorial Assistant: Jennifer Jones
Production: Jill Macey

First published in 1992 by
Conran Octopus Limited,
37 Shelton Street, London WC2H 9HN

British Library Cataloguing in Publication Data

Wills, Judith
Slim and healthy Mediterranean cooking.
I. Title
641.591822

ISBN 1 85029 370 8

Typeset by Flairplan
Printed and bound in Singapore

CONTENTS

FOOD FOR THOUGHT

In this first chapter we look at the way Western man's diet has changed over the centuries and at the strong evidence which points to why today's Western diet is so bad for our health, while the simple diet traditional in Mediterranean countries is the ideal way for us all to eat for many reasons.

For most of the existence of the human species – around 50,000 years – we have lived on a diet consisting largely of unrefined plant foods, such as leaves, seeds, nuts and fruits, supplemented by a little meat or fish when it was successfully hunted. Farmed grains were added to the diet after the first agricultural revolution about 10,000 years ago.

Anthropologists estimate that throughout all of that time, the total fat content of the human diet was no more than about 20%.

A mere 200 years ago, at the start of the Industrial Revolution, the diet of people in the new urban areas of industrial concentration began to change. The resulting changes since have been so drastic that in Western Europe and the USA our diet now consists of around 40% fat, and our consumption of unrefined plant foods has been halved. Instead, 'simple carbohydrates' as sugars – virtually unknown to us 200 years ago – now form about 20% of our every-day diet.

Faced with the evidence of such major dietary change in such a relatively very tiny time span, it is easy to see how the modern Western diet could be a major cause of modern Western ills. Heart diseases, stroke and cancer between them now account for over 70% of all deaths in the USA and industrialized Northern Europe.

The problem of having too much to eat has rapidly overtaken the problem of finding enough to eat. Obesity and related problems, such as mid-life diabetes, are now serious epidemics; whereas diseases related to malnutrition, like scurvy and rickets for example, have all but disappeared.

Interestingly, however, the people of the less industrialized areas of the Mediterranean have not succumbed to the sort of high-fat, highly-refined diet so prevalent in other areas. These 'Mediterraneans' eat a diet which contains a balance of nutrients very similar to that of our ancestors. Their low rates of heart disease and cancer and

OPPOSITE: breakfast of fresh fruit, fruit juice, crusty bread and Greek-style Yogurt (page 124)

their longer life expectancy are surely the proof that a prudent diet is the best life insurance we can buy.

Many worldwide cross-cultural studies and an increasing amount of scientific evidence can leave us in little doubt, as we head to the twenty-first century, that what we eat affects our health. If we eat unwisely, we are putting ourselves at unnecessary risk; if we eat wisely we can actually protect ourselves and increase our chances of living longer and healthier lives.

The good news is that, through decades of research into the specific causes of disease, it is now possible for us to be sure of what really constitutes a 'healthy diet'. This is true both in terms of the amounts of the different food groups we should eat, what we should cut down on for example, and in terms of particular individual foods that can offer us real 'health protection' – in other words, foods we should eat more of. The traditional diet of the people who live in the countries bordering the Mediterranean comes closer than any other modern diet to matching this dietary ideal.

DIET AND DISORDER

Before looking at the Mediterranean diet in detail, let us examine more closely the current Western European diet and its links with the 'diseases of affluence', as some now call heart disease, cancer, diabetes, obesity and other disorders.

FATS

The link between a diet high in fat, particularly saturated fat, and increased risk of heart disease, strokes and some forms of cancer is now definitely proven by medical research fundings.

There are three types of fat in our diet:
SATURATED FAT is found mainly in animal produce and it is that type of fat which tends to be solid at room temperature. Butter, lard, suet and the fat you see on cuts of meat are all high in saturates. The fat in dairy produce is high in saturates too, as are many margarines. However, the only plant to contain a lot of saturated fat is the coconut.
POLYUNSATURATED FAT is usually found in vegetable oils which are mostly liquid at normal room

NUTRIENTS	1 WHAT WE EAT NOW PERCENTAGE OF DAILY FOOD CALORIE INTAKE	2 WHAT WE SHOULD EAT* PERCENTAGE OF DAILY FOOD CALORIE INTAKE	
		LOWER LIMIT	UPPER LIMIT
TOTAL FATS	42%	15%	30%
BROKEN DOWN AS:			
SATURATED FATS	27%	NO LOWER LIMIT	10%
POLYUNSATURATED	7%	3%	7%
MONO-UNSATURATED	8%	To make up the difference between combined total of saturated and poly-unsaturated fats and total fat intake, ie between 12% and 13%	
PROTEIN	15–20%	10%	15%
TOTAL CARBOHYDRATES	40–45%	55%	75%
BROKEN DOWN AS:			
SIMPLE CARBOHYDRATES (SUGARS)	20%	0%	10%
COMPLEX CARBOHYDRATES	20–25%	50%	70%
FIBRE	20 g	27 g	40 g
SALT	12 g	NOT DETERMINED**	6 g

All figures are approximate and average.
* As outlined in 'Diet, Nutrition and the Prevention of Chronic Diseases'
(World Health Organization 1990)
** In Britain the daily lower limit for salt is generally considered as 3 g.

temperature. Oils high in polyunsaturates are corn oil, sunflower oil, and safflower oil. Polyunsaturated margarines are made from these oils. Oily fish, such as mackerel, sardines and herring, are also high in polyunsaturates.

MONO-UNSATURATED FAT is contained in the highest amounts in olive oil, peanut (groundnut) oil and rapeseed oil.

No one source of fat is 100% saturated, polyunsaturated or mono-unsaturated. For instance, red meat contains as much poly- and mono- (combined) as it does saturated fat, and only about half the fat in corn oil is polyunsaturated.

Unfortunately, the main source of fat in our diets now is not natural basic foods, such as a slice of roast beef or a spoonful of oil, but the high amount of convenience, packeted foods that we consume. Cakes, pastries, biscuits, chocolates, food mixes, packet desserts and oven chips are some of the most obvious items on an endless list of the foods that many of us now regard as normal eating and which are providing us with our huge fat intake without many of us being really aware of it.

By the 1950s coronary heart disease (CHD) had become the single major cause of death in Britain and the USA. The relationship between diet and CHD was most famously supported by the Seven Countries Study published in 1980, when it was discovered that high levels of saturated fat intake and blood cholesterol in some countries almost exactly matched those with the highest levels of death from CHD.

Saturated fat in the diet raises blood cholesterol levels which leads to 'furring' of the arteries so that the blood literally has difficulty in circulating round the body. The cholesterol also forms into clots which cause strokes and heart attacks. Saturated fats contribute to this effect by stimulating the production of 'low density lipoproteins' which encourage the depositing of cholesterol.

A diet rich in cholesterol – foods such as eggs, liver and some shellfish – also raises blood cholesterol. However, for the average person, the real problem is saturated fat.

In the Seven Countries Study, Japan had the lowest saturated fat intake at 3% and blood cholesterol was low at 4.3, while in Finland, saturated fat intake was 22% and blood cholesterol high at 7.0. CHD deaths over the 15-year period of the study were 144 per 10,000 in Japan – but an alarming 1,202 per 10,000 in Finland!

This study was just one of many international studies to produce results clearly linking saturated fat and high blood cholesterol with CHD.

Diets high in the other types of fat do not produce a similar link. The Eskimos, who eat a diet very high in polyunsaturated fish oils, have a low rate of CHD. The same is true of the peoples of the poorer areas of the Mediterranean, such as Greece and Southern Italy, who eat a diet reasonably high in fat in the form of olive oil, yet have CHD death rates around *half* that of Britain and the USA.

A diet high in saturated fat is also linked with increased risk of some forms of cancer, particularly colon cancer, prostate cancer and breast cancer. According to the World Health Organization, other diseases and conditions that are made worse by eating the typical Western affluent diet include: diabetes, obesity, diverticulitis, gallstones, haemorrhoids, constipation and arthritis.

PROTEIN

In the late, '50s, '60s and '70s, most people's main nutritional worry was whether or not they were getting enough protein in their diet. A meal wasn't regarded as a 'proper' meal unless it contained a large visible portion of an animal protein, such as meat, eggs, fish or poultry.

In fact, we now know that a diet containing as little as 10% protein is adequate and that eating more than about 15% is totally unnecessary. Also, the source of protein doesn't need to be animal. There was much talk in these same decades about 'high quality' and 'low quality' protein. Although it was known that many plant foods contain good amounts of protein, they were considered inferior to animal sources. We now know that plant sources, such as beans and lentils, are every bit as good as the protein in a slab of beef.

In Britain especially, many people also tend to get their protein from convenience foods and/or fatty cuts of meat which also contain high proportions of fat, eg fish deep-fried in batter, hamburgers or meat pies and pasties.

CARBOHYDRATES

The typical diet in Britain and the USA, high in fat and protein, is correspondingly relatively low in carbohydrates – ie the foods of plant origin, such as cereals, pulses, nuts, seeds, fruit and vegetables. Much of the carbohydrate that we do eat is also refined carbohydrate – sugary products which contain little fibre and, often to make matters worse, a great deal of fat.

As Table 1 shows, virtually half of all the carbohydrate we eat is in the form of sugar, ie 'empty calories' containing no nutrients at all: no vitamins or minerals, no protein, no fibre – just calories! We each eat on average about 980 g/2 lb of sugar every week, or about 125 g/4½ oz (more than 22 teaspoonfuls) every day! Half of this is bought in packets for use at home; the other half is eaten as sweets, cakes, biscuits, chocolates and in canned and other commercially processed foods.

If we are to eat as the WHO recommends in Table 2, there is, however, room for only 5% of our daily calories to be in the form of sugar. (If you are eating up to 30% of calories as fat, 15% as protein and 50% minimum as complex, ie unrefined, carbohydrates, that adds up to 95%.) 5% of the average daily diet of 2,000 calories equals 100 calories – or about 25 g/1 oz of sugar a day, which is only about 5 teaspoonfuls.

The real problem with a diet that relies a lot on convenience and packet foods is that it is very hard to know exactly how much sugar you *are* eating. However, a diet high in natural unprocessed foods means it is a simple task to limit your added sugar intake. You can then happily add a little sugar or honey to your breakfast yogurt, knowing that you are well within the 5% limit.

FIBRE

The typical Western high-fat, high-protein, low-carbohydrate diet also contains too little fibre. The term fibre covers several different types of non-digestible substances found in our diet and present only in plant foods. There is no fibre in animal produce and none in fat. A diet low in fibre is linked with an increased risk of colon cancer, diabetes mellitus, and of diverticulitis and a wide-range of other digestive disorders.

SALT

As a diet high in salt is linked with high blood pressure and an increased likelihood of high blood pressure and heart disease later in life, the WHO recommends an upper limit of 6 g a day – about half the intake of many of us at the moment.

Of the salt we eat, about one-third is present in foods naturally; another third is added in cooking and at the table, and the final third is consumed in commercially prepared foods, such as crisps, cereals, canned vegetables, canned meats, pickles and in take-aways and convenience meals.

It is therefore quite easy to see that if we switch to a diet which eliminates most refined convenience foods and if we stop adding salt indiscriminately at the table, we can easily achieve the 6 g target and still use a little salt in cooking.

TOWARDS A HEALTHIER DIET

If we are to cut down on fats, especially saturated fats, and on sugar, and if we are to eat no more protein than we do at present, how are we then to make up the shortfall in calories that this will present – assuming, of course, that we don't want to lose weight! The answer is simply more complex carbohydrates: more grains, such as bread, breakfast cereals, rice, pasta etc; more pulses, such as beans, peas, lentils; more root vegetables, like potatoes, sweet potatoes and beets; more nuts and seeds, and more fresh fruit and other vegetables.

At present, as Table 1 shows, these foods form no more than 25% of our diet, whereas, as Table 2 shows, the WHO recommends they should constitute at least 50%. Not only do these complex carbohydrates have *no negative effects* – there are no links between them and diseases or ills of any kind – they also have plenty of positive effects. Not only do they provide quantities of fibres for bowel regularity, and have a high content of the various vitamins and minerals we need for good health, but we also now know they offer real, *positive*, protective benefits. These benefits will be discussed in more detail in the next chapter.

The question of complex carbohydrates brings us back to the diet of the Mediterraneans – a diet that relies first on carbohydrates and only to a very small extent on animal produce.

Though the Mediterranean countries vary in their preferred foods and styles of cooking – for instance, Italy is the home of pasta and salads, while Moroccans eat more grains, spices and dried fruits – the overall balance of nutrients works out remarkably similarly in all the Mediterranean countries. This balance tallies almost perfectly with the WHO ideals as set out in Table 2.

Some of the Mediterranean people do, of course, love their rich desserts and pastries. Traditionally, however, these have been eaten only rarely. They are usually reserved for feast days and celebrations, and are certainly not eaten on a regular daily basis.

Let us examine some of the differences between the daily diet of an average Briton and that of a Mediterranean person.

BREAKFAST

The British cooked breakfast is still a strong feature. Although the fry-up of sausages, bacon and egg is not now eaten as regularly as it once was, it is still a normal element of weekend life in Britain. Even on a day without a cooked breakfast the average Briton will have thickly buttered toast and put full cream milk in coffee or tea. Moreover, in certain areas of Britain, particularly Scotland and the North of England, the cooked breakfast still reigns.

The Mediterranean breakfast rarely involves anything cooked. It is a high-complex-carbohydrate affair – crusty bread, some fruit preserves (butter is rarely used), some fresh fruit and/or fruit juice is typical throughout the area. There may sometimes also be yogurt – a low-fat source of easily digested protein. In current nutritional terms, the Mediterranean breakfast is a perfect start to the day.

LUNCH

If the Briton is eating at home, he or she may well make up for the lack of a cooked breakfast with a sausage and egg meal at lunchtime instead. Alternatively, a can of soup may be opened or an omelette made. If trying to 'be good' and watching their weight, he or she will perhaps have a portion of chicken with a small side salad consisting of a few lettuce leaves with a little thinly sliced cucumber and tomato. To this he or she will probably add some mayonnaise, not realizing it is a very high-fat, high-calorie food.

If eating in the office or on the run, they will buy a sandwich (often of white bread) filled with Cheddar cheese or high-fat corned beef – or have a take-away hamburger. There may also be a chocolate bar or a slice of cake to follow.

The Mediterranean lunch snack is more likely to be home-made soup, usually based on vegetables or pulses, a plate of cooked beans or a grain such as bulgar dressed with a little olive oil, or some fresh sardines with plenty of crusty whole grain bread and a big salad. Alternatively, there may be a selection of stuffed vegetables or dips and spreads to accompany flat bread - and *always* a salad.

MAIN MEAL

When the British cook for their families, they first work out what meat or poultry, or other protein source, will form the centrepiece of the meal, and

then rather casually decide what vegetable will go with it as an after-thought. Potatoes or some white rice will usually feature, but very often any other vegetable is out of a can or is a small portion of some – often over-boiled – greenery: tinned carrots or peas are the norm. There is often a fat-laden dessert – apple pie and gateaux are currently the two most popular desserts in Britain for adults – and children eat ice-cream and instant packet desserts literally by the ton.

When the Mediterraneans sit down to their main meal of the day, it will most probably be based around a grain, and it will often be a vegetarian meal: perhaps tomato sauce added to pasta, or mushrooms added to rice. There will always also be a variety of vegetables or salad, either in the dish or to accompany it, and fresh fruit afterwards.

Because of the scarcity of red meat in the poorer areas of the Mediterranean, it was reserved for special occasions, and many people saw lamb, say, only once or twice a year. Instead, poultry and fish are the two main sources of animal protein. Animal foods are also 'stretched', ie used in small quantities as a part of a carbohydrate-based meal. High protein pulses are mostly used in their stead.

Without even realizing it, the people of the Mediterranean have been following the kind of diet that the WHO now recommends we all adopt.

Ironically, as the development of the EEC and growing industrialization of rural areas of the Mediterranean increase local awareness of how the citizens of Germany, Britain and the USA eat – and as fast-food outlets spring up all over – the villagers of the Mediterranean are beginning to adopt the Western diet themselves. Sadly they, too, are seeing an increase in heart disease and cancer.

However, they have a long way to go to catch up. The average life expectancy of an Italian man is nearly two years longer than that of a Briton. If Italian health care, expenditure and facilities had been comparable to that of Britain over the past 50 years or so, I have no doubt that this gap would be even wider.

Celery and Artichoke Salad (page 109); mixed leaf salad; Vegetable Lasagne (page 96); Melon and Strawberry Salad (page 121)

PROTECTION ON A PLATE

Changing to a really healthy diet means not only cutting down on fats and refined foods and eating much more fibre, but also eating certain  'protective' foods. Here we look in detail at such foods – from olive oil to pulses, fruits and vegetables – all abundant in the Mediterranean region.

The first stage in establishing a healthy diet is to get the balance of nutrients right, as outlined in the previous chapter.

However, there have also been new and exciting developments in health/diet research in the last decade as a result of work done around the world by scientists investigating the idea that certain foods actually protect our health.

Including such foods – or, perhaps, including more of them – in the diet actually seems to help protect the body from all kinds of diseases and problems. The risks of developing heart disease, high blood pressure, strokes, some forms of cancer and digestive disorders can now be greatly reduced, it would seem, by these 'protective foods'.

Interestingly, some foods actually contain more than one of the 'protective factors': broccoli, spinach, peaches, garlic, broad beans …if there is such a thing as a group of 'superfoods', then perhaps these, and a few others, are they.

It is precisely these foods, and the others discussed in this chapter, that form the basis of the diet of the Mediterraneans. The grains, the pulses, the fruits and vegetables – even the olive oil and wine – which are the staples of the area provide what now appears to be the ultimate healthy diet.

This chapter examines the protective factors in question, all of which can be easily adapted for a Western diet and palate, with all the same benefits. Benefits that can work in as short a time as a few months to improve your health, reduce the risk of ill health in the future, and enhance life expectancy.

NOT ALL FATS ARE BAD

In its recommendations on how we should lower our intake of fats to help prevent coronary heart disease and other ills, the World Health Organization suggests that we should cut our intake of saturated fats by at least half – from levels currently at 20% plus (of total energy intake) down to a maximum of 10%.

OPPOSITE: Sultana-baked Sardines (page 80)

15

Although a diet high in polyunsaturated fats can lower blood cholesterol, it suggests that we should not increase our intake of these fats from the current maximum intake of 7%. Their logic regarding this appears to be that if our intake of saturated fats is reduced sufficiently, a 7% intake of polyunsaturates will be enough to maintain reduced blood cholesterol levels.

Interestingly, however, the WHO is quite happy for us to increase our intake of mono–unsaturated fats. It doesn't actually specify a maximum intake but by implication that figure is 13% (total recommended fat intake is 30%, saturates maximum 10%, polyunsaturates maximum 7%, leaving 13% for mono-unsaturates). Current mono-unsaturate intake levels are estimated at between 7 and 10%.

Olive oil is the most widely used oil containing a high proportion of mono-unsaturates, the only other being peanut (groundnut) oil. Olive oil is, of course, the most favoured cooking oil in the Mediterranean. Although butter and other fats and oils are used occasionally, it is the native oil of Greece, Italy and Spain and features at virtually every Mediterranean meal.

Because of their capacity to lower blood cholesterol, the polyunsaturated fats have received the most attention and the most funds for research over the past 15 years or so. However, the mono-unsaturates are just as interesting. In fact, worldwide, experts are now beginning to realize that they may be even more beneficial to our health.

In every trial conducted with olive oil so far, it has been shown to have an equally strong capacity to lower blood cholesterol. It also appears to have two very important advantages over polyunsaturates in this respect.

Firstly, a diet high in cholesterol-lowering polyunsaturates but very low in other fats has been shown in trials to have an unfortunate tendency to decrease the levels of the 'good for you' High Density Lipoproteins (HDLs) as well as lowering the levels of 'bad for you' Low Density Lipoproteins (LDLs), which encourage the levels of blood cholesterol to rise.

Secondly, a diet high in polyunsaturates also appears to increase the risk of some forms of cancer. Scientists believe that this is probably because polyunsaturates are very vulnerable to free radical attack, according to a report published in the leading British medical publication, 'The Lancet', in 1991. In other words, they are easily oxidized in our bodies and this means that cell mutations which may lead to the beginnings of cancers may be more easily formed. More work is being done on the exact nature and extent of these links.

In trials, mono-unsaturated oils have been shown to reduce the cholesterol-encouraging LDLs by up to 21% – while not affecting the beneficial HDLs. Also, because of its different molecular structure, mono-unsaturated oil is not subject to oxidation in the body. In other words, olive oil appears to lower LDLs and blood cholesterol levels *without* any possible harmful side effects. Meanwhile, the Mediterraneans, who eat a diet relatively high in olive oil but low in saturated fat, have heart disease levels about half those of the British.

Olive oil also offers protection in other areas. It is the most easily digested of fats, and taking it regularly has been shown to improve over half of all stomach ulcers, probably by reducing bile acids and stimulating the action of the pancreas.

It is also likely that a regular intake of olive oil may keep you looking, and feeling, younger for longer. Olive oil may protect you from high levels of the 'free radicals' which experts now believe are the major cause of the ageing process in humans. 'Free radicals' and their action will be examined in more detail later in the chapter.

There is one other type of oil that is of particular benefit in protecting us against heart disease. This is the special type of polyunsaturated oil found in fish, especially oily fish such as sardines, mackerel and tuna – the fish of the Mediterranean.

This particular oil contains 'Omega-3' fatty acids which have remarkable powers to lower LDLs and blood cholesterol, as well as having other benefits on the circulatory system. The Omega-3s have such a powerful effect in this respect that a mere two portions of oily fish a week can offer real protection.

Although fish is not a cheap commodity in the Mediterranean, it is still eaten on a regular basis, especially the more plentiful fish such as sardines and mackerel. It is certainly eaten more frequently than red meat and even poultry. Mediterraneans also eat a lot of canned fish, such as anchovies, sardines and tuna, which still retain the Omega-3s, and no doubt contribute to their well-being.

COMPLEX CARBOHYDRATES

As we saw in the previous chapter, the Mediterranean diet is made up of a high proportion of complex carbohydrates, such as grains, pulses, root vegetables, nuts and seeds, fruits and vegetables. As well as being able to restore the correct fat/protein/carbohydrate balance to our diets, these complex carbohydrates also offer another major benefit in that they contain different types of fibre.

We all know about 'roughage', the insoluble fibre contained in bran, for instance, which helps to keep our digestive systems functioning well. However, many complex carbohydrate foods also contain another special sort of fibre which is soluble in water. Being water-soluble, this type of fibre doesn't have the same effect on our digestive systems, but it *does* have one very important effect – it lowers blood cholesterol levels.

A few years ago it appeared that oats were the main source of soluble fibre, but it is now known that the pulses – all the dried beans, peas and lentils – are an even richer source and have an even better ability to lower blood cholesterol. Latest research trials have shown that eating small portions of pulses, between 25 g/1 oz and 140 g/5 oz per day, lowers blood cholesterol by between 7% and 26%, depending on the individual's starting level.

Also, while the effect of soluble fibre is to lower bad LDLs, the good HDLs stay the same. In other words, soluble fibre has a very similar effect to foods such as olive oil and fish oils in helping to stave off heart disease. The Mediterranean diet has always relied heavily on pulses of all kinds as a source both of carbohydrate and of protein.

In addition, a diet high in complex carbohydrates also offers protection from some cancers. According to the WHO, 'Diets high in plant foods …are associated with a lower occurence of cancers. Although the mechanisms underlying these effects are not fully understood, such diets are usually low in saturated fat and high in starches and fibre.'

More research is being done into the benefits of a diet high in complex carbohydrates. Meanwhile it is prudent to aim for that 55% level of the Mediterranean villagers.

FRUITS AND VEGETABLES

Fruits and vegetables are part of the carbohydrate group of foods. They contain simple carbohydrates, such as fructose (fruit sugar) in fruits for instance, and various types of fibre including the soluble fibre pectin. They also contain some starch: either a very little, as in lettuce; or a lot, as in bananas.

At the moment, we eat only about 200 g/7 oz of fruit or vegetables a day, excluding root vegetables, and the WHO would like that at least to double.

This is not only because all fruits and vegetables are a good source of fibre and the vitamins and minerals which we need regularly for good health and as a protection against deficiency diseases. It also appears that certain vitamins and vitamin-like substances contained in many fruits and vegetables offer real protection against heart disease and certain forms of cancer.

The key vitamins are vitamins C and E, and beta-carotene, a 'pro-vitamin' which converts to vitamin A in our bodies. At one time it was thought that this pro-vitamin was simply a way of obtaining vitamin A, but it now appears to have very special properties that vitamin A from other sources, such as dairy produce, simply does not have.

Fruits and vegetables containing most vitamin C per portion are: citrus fruits, especially oranges; peppers of all colours; broccoli; parsley; Brussels sprouts; all leafy green vegetables; strawberries; guava; mango; melon; and tomatoes. All fruits and vegetables contain some vitamin C.

Foods rich in vitamin E are: vegetable oils including olive oil; nuts; seeds; whole grains; leafy green vegetables; and avocados.

Best sources of beta-carotene are: all yellow, orange and dark green vegetables, such as carrots, sweet potatoes, pumpkins, spinach, broccoli, watercress, dark lettuce leaves, tomatoes, asparagus, peas, cabbage, sweetcorn; and yellow and orange fruits, such as mangoes, melons, apricots, peaches, nectarines and oranges.

OVERLEAF: a selection of Mediterranean
fruits and vegetables

As you can see, most of these fruits and vegetables appear time and again in the diet of the Mediterraneans.

What exactly is so special about these three vitamins? They are 'anti-oxidants' and are important in our diets because they appear to 'scavenge' or inactivate the free radicals which are constantly being produced in our bodies and which can damage cells and tissues by oxidation. If the body's level of anti-oxidants is low, free radicals 'run wild' – and trouble can start. The genetic material of cells may be altered, leading to cancerous states.

According to WHO statistics, an increased intake of fruits and vegetables is linked to a decreased rate of colon cancer, rectal cancer, stomach cancer, and cervical cancer. The latest research from a joint study in France and Singapore also indicates a reduced risk of breast cancer.

Low levels of beta-carotene intake, in particular, are linked with a high risk of lung cancer and oral cancers. Many experts also agree that the anti-oxidant vitamins have a large role to play in preventing heart disease because it may be the oxidation of LDLs by free radicals which causes the narrowing of the arteries.

Lastly, the anti-oxidant vitamins may also play a part in reducing the effects of ageing. The Gerentology Research Centre in the USA claims a 'great deal of experimental evidence' on this, suggesting that people who increase their intake of the anti-oxidants will age more slowly and delay the onset of diseases associated with old age.

To conclude, the WHO says in its report, 'Diet, Nutrition and the Prevention of Chronic Diseases':

'A substantial amount of epidemiological and clinical data indicates that a high intake of plant foods and complex carbohydrates is associated with a reduced risk of several chronic diseases, especially coronary heart disease, certain cancers, hypertension (high blood pressure) and diabetes.'

GARLIC

Much-loved by the Mediterraneans for centuries and much ignored elsewhere, garlic has for years had a reputation as a 'miracle cure' for all kinds of ills. Many of these were thought 'old wives' tales', but garlic's power as an antiseptic and antifungal agent are medically proven. Now, it would also seem that a clove or two of garlic a day can help us to health in other ways.

Research has now shown that garlic's active ingredient, allicin, helps to prevent blood clots from forming by dilating blood vessels and by reducing the 'stickiness' of blood. Garlic also lowers blood cholesterol levels *and* it also destroys free radicals. Finally, it can reduce high blood pressure.

All in all, if there really is a 'miracle' health food, garlic may perhaps be it! Experts believe that one or two cloves a day are enough to offer protection.

Garlic grows wild in the Mediterranean region and is added to very many of the classic dishes of the area – not because the Mediterraneans knew something we didn't know about the bulb, but simply because they liked the taste!

Onions and other members of the garlic and onion family, such as leeks and chives, probably have a similar, but less potent, healthy effect.

WINE

The Mediterraneans drink wine in preference to any other alcoholic drink, because grapes are abundant and wine is easy to make. It also tastes good with meals – which is how the Mediterraneans prefer to do their drinking!

The British Heart Foundation and many other expert bodies now agree that moderate alcohol consumption may actually be good for your heart and your health. 'A concensus is growing for a beneficial effect,' said the BHF in 1991.

Although no one disagrees that over-indulgence of any type of alcoholic is *bad* for your health, up to two glasses of wine a day for women and three for men appear to offer some protection against heart disease by lowering the tendency for the blood to clot.

Sixteen different trials have come to the conclusion that moderate alcohol intake is of benefit. Wine is also an aid to digestion when taken with a meal, as it stimulates the hormones involved in the digestive processes, and it is a relaxant.

If, like the Mediterraneans, you enjoy a glass or two of wine with your meal, perhaps it is time to stop feeling guilty.

OPPOSITE: Olive Oil and Garlic Sauce (page 101)

BALANCING YOUR DIET

Now for the practicalities! Let us discover how to turn your new-found nutritional knowledge into a healthy diet which will not only really work for you, but will fit easily into your own existing life-style and which – above all – you and your friends and family will really enjoy.

How do you put all these new nutritional ideas into practice? How do you make them part of a daily diet that will not only keep you healthy and fit, but that you will find attractive and easy to live with?

Be assured that you will not have to spend your life consulting nutrition manuals, or carrying a calculator round with you in the supermarket to make sure that every meal is perfectly balanced. Common sense is the most important tool.

Firstly, I suggest that you make changes gradually. This is partly for your convenience and partly because a digestive system that has been used to a low-fibre, low-fruit and vegetable, high-fat way of eating needs a little time to adjust. In particular I think it is a good idea to build up slowly your intake of pulses, such as peas, beans and lentils.

After a few weeks, the Mediterranean-style of eating will become second nature to you and you will find you are shopping and eating in a healthier way without even thinking about it. Interestingly enough, should you *then* try to revert to the high-fat, low-carbohydrate way of eating, your digestive system would protest even more.

THE ENERGY TRIANGLE

Let us recap on the three sources of energy (calories) in your diet, and how much of each type you should be eating.

PROTEIN is needed to build and repair lean tissue: muscles, organs, nerves and so on. About 15% of our calories should come from protein. In an average diet of 2,000 calories a day, that represents 300 calories, or 75 g/3 oz of pure protein.

CARBOHYDRATE we need to give us energy. *At least* 55% of what we eat should be carbohydrates, but eating more than this won't do you any harm. The 'starchy' carbohydrates, such as bread, potatoes, pasta and rice, are the foods to 'fill up on' when you are hungry, rather than adding extra animal produce to your diet.

OPPOSITE: red mullet; sardines; tomatoes and broad beans

23

The only carbohydrates to worry about keeping to a minimum in your diet are highly refined carbohydrates, such as sugar and sugary products. Alcohol consumption also needs to be moderate.

By following the recipes and plans in this book you can be assured that your refined carbohydrate intake will be much lower than levels recommended by both the British Government and the World Health Organization.

On a diet of 2,000 calories per day, your carbohydrate intake should be at least 1,100 calories – or 275 g/10 oz of pure carbohydrate.

FATS AND OILS form the remainder of your calories. That is, up to 30%, 600 calories or 67 g/2½ oz of fat. This is a maximum and in theory you could get as little as 10% of your daily calories in the form of fat and still stay in perfect health. In practice, however, a little fat makes other foods more palatable and, as fat is present in so many natural foods, it is extremely hard to lower intake to below 10–20%.

Of this fat, a good balance to aim for is a maximum of about 10% saturated fat, and the other 20% will be made up of mono-unsaturated fats, such as olive oil, and polyunsaturated fats, such as corn oil.

It is also important to realize that few foods contain only one of the three calorie-givers, that is are all protein, or all carbohydrates or all fat. Most foods are a mixture. For instance, meat and cheese are regarded as 'protein' foods, but even lean meat contains around 10% fat and Cheddar cheese 30%.

For this reason it is best to go for the lower-fat sources of protein most of the time. These include: white fish; shellfish; eggs; low-fat cheeses, such as those soft cheeses made from skimmed milk, and medium-fat soft cheeses such as Feta and Brie. The Italians love Parmesan cheese which *is* a high-fat cheese; grated, however, a little goes a long way. Chicken and rabbit are excellent low-fat meats and *lean* lamb, beef and pork are perfectly acceptable sources of protein, if eaten in moderation.

High-carbohydrate foods often also contain both protein and fat. For instance, potatoes are a high-carbohydrate food (about 90%) and the rest is mostly protein and a trace of fat.

The complex carbohydrates are all reasonable sources of protein. But those highest in protein are pulses of all kinds, which contain around 30% protein and little or no fat. Nuts are also a source of both carbohydrates and protein.

All this means is that you need only consume small amounts of the animal 'protein foods' to stay healthy. Being careful with the animal sources of protein, especially dairy produce, will also lower your saturated fat intake.

VARIETY IS THE KEY
Once you have understood the main need for more carbohydrates and less fat in your diet, perhaps the single most important watchword for healthy eating is simply *variety*.

The easiest way to get all the nutrients you need for health, especially all the vitamins and minerals, is to eat a wide variety of different types of food from within both the high-carbohydrate and high-protein groups. That is because foods of a similar protein or carbohydrate content vary enormously as to their content of vital vitamins and minerals.

Let us compare two high-carbohydrate foods: rice and potatoes. Assuming portion sizes containing a similar number of calories, the potato contains more fibre and potassium, while the rice contains more protein, zinc and some B vitamins.

Now let us look at two common high-protein foods: chicken and white fish. The chicken is a good source of niacin, while the fish contains more vitamin E and folic acid.

There are hundreds more examples of this sort and it is for this reason that no one food is 'the best'. *Eat a variety of foods for optimum health!*
● Make a high-carbohydrate food the main part of at least two meals each day, and at least some part of the third meal of the day.
● Include fresh fruits and vegetables or salads at *every* meal, or nearly every meal. Be sure to eat as many red, orange and yellow fruits and vegetables and leafy green vegetables as you can.
● Eat pulses regularly as the main part of a meal, and use a little nuts and/or seeds every day – they can simply be sprinkled on other foods.

THE RECIPES
The recipes in the book all have a nutrition panel which I will explain in a little more detail here.

SATURATED FAT is listed as 'low', 'medium' or 'high'. 'Low' means less than 5% of the total energy content of that recipe; 'medium' denotes 5–15%, and 'high' is over 15%. However, *no recipe in this book is truly high in saturated fat* or it would not be included. The maximum I have allowed is 20%.

If you choose a recipe with a medium or high saturated fat content, it makes sense to match it with a very low-fat accompaniment. All the complex carbohydrates contain very little fat, as do fresh fruit and leafy vegetables.

PROTEIN content is also listed 'low', 'medium' or 'high'. 'Low' means under 15% of total energy; 'medium' denotes 15–20% and 'high' over 20%. If you choose a low-protein dish, say *Stuffed Peppers*, for one meal, pick a high-protein dish at another time in the day. Alternatively, combine a low-protein dish, such as *Mushrooms in Garlic Sauce*, with a high-protein dish at the same meal.

CARBOHYDRATE content is also listed 'low', 'medium' or 'high'. 'Low' means under 50% of total energy; 'medium' denotes 50-60% and 'high' is over 60%. Some people would consider that a meal containing, say, 49% carbohydrate *is not* low in carbohydrate at all. However, as I am aiming to get your carbohydrate intake up to at least 55% of your total calorie intake, in my terms under 50% *is* low. So the same rule applies: balance any low-carbohydrate dish with a high-carbohydrate accompaniment, and include at least two high-carbohydrate dishes each day.

FIBRE content is listed in grams. You should try to eat at least 25 g of fibre each day, preferably 30 g. Remember that you will be getting fibre not just from the recipes but also from accompanying bread, vegetables, salads and fruit, etc. The only foods that do not contain fibre are animal products and highly refined produce such as sugar.

CHOLESTEROL content of the recipes is listed for those who have been advised to cut down the cholesterol in their diets by their doctor. For most of us, however, it is more important to watch intake of saturated fat than cholesterol. A maximum of 300 mg a day is perfectly acceptable for everyone. Eggs and shellfish, while being low in fat *are* high in cholesterol, so it is wise not to have more than one egg or shellfish dish in any one day.

VITAMINS AND MINERALS are listed where most abundant in each recipe in order of quantity. Virtually all the recipes will also contain traces of many other nutrients, but if a particular vitamin or mineral is listed it means that this recipe is a particularly good source of it. Watch out especially for recipes high in vitamins C, A (including beta-carotene), E, the B group – B1, B2, niacin, B6, B12 and folic acid – and for dishes rich in iron and calcium.

Salt is optional in most recipes and I recommend that you use as little as you find palatable. If you have been used to a diet high in salt it is worth retraining your taste-buds to accept less, something the Mediterranean diet can help you to do easily as the profusion of herbs, garlic and spices add flavour without the need for salt.

THE PLANS

If you look through the menu plans which follow you will see the 'variety' theme working well.

The plans in this chapter are constructed to supply around 2,000 calories a day, which is a reasonable figure for most moderately active women. *Men* will probably need extra, which they should get by increasing intake of complex carbohydrates with, perhaps, a little more higher-protein food, such as poultry, low-fat cheeses or fish.

Wherever a plan includes one of the recipes from the book (indicated in italics), it obviously refers to a single portion (one quarter of the total) and quantities should be adjusted accordingly.

SPECIAL NEEDS

Vegetarians and vegans will find plenty of suitable recipes, especially in the chapters on Starters, Soups and Snacks; Suppers and Lunches; Pasta and Grains and, of course, Salads and Vegetables. I have also devised both a maintenance plan and a low-calorie plan for vegetarians.

Vegetarians should make sure to eat plenty of dishes rich in the B vitamins, protein, iron and calcium. Pulses are the best source of protein for vegans, who eat no animal produce at all.

Children will also enjoy the Mediterranean style of diet. They often have quite high calorie needs for their age and height, and they also need plenty of protein and calcium to build bone and muscle.

BUSY SINGLES

QUICK AND CONVENIENT EATING FOR PEOPLE ON THEIR OWN AND IN A HURRY.
ABOUT 2,000 CALORIES PER DAY

Extras per day: 250 ml/8 fl oz skimmed milk, 2 glasses of wine (optional).

DAY ONE

BREAKFAST
140 ml/¼ pt fresh fruit juice of
choice
2 slices of bread with a little low-fat
spread and honey or pure fruit spread

LUNCH
Prawn salad
slice of melon or 1 banana

EVENING
Tzatziki with a selection of crudités
Rice with Peppers and Pork
140 ml/¼ pt *Greek-style Yogurt*
2 apricots or 25 g/1 oz dried fruit

DAY TWO

BREAKFAST
2 pieces of fresh fruit of choice
200 ml/7 fl oz *Greek-style Yogurt*
25 g/1 oz muesli

LUNCH
Tunisian Eggs
50 g/2 oz bread
50 g/2 oz vanilla ice-cream
1 apple or orange

EVENING
1 large red mullet or medium
mackerel, grilled with lemon juice
and black pepper
Puréed Potatoes
Spinach with Oil and Garlic

DAY THREE

BREAKFAST
25 g/1 oz dried dates or apricots
140 ml/¼ pt *Greek-style Yogurt*
140 ml/¼ pt fresh fruit juice of
choice
25 g/1 oz slice of bread with pure
fruit spread

LUNCH
slice of melon or 1 peach or
nectarine
Pasta Crunch
25 g/1 oz slice of bread

EVENING
1 pork chop, trimmed of all visible
fat and grilled
Red Pepper and Chilli Sauce
Carrot and Potato Purée
French Beans in Orange Sauce

DAY FOUR

BREAKFAST
1 wholemeal bread roll with low-fat
spread and pure fruit spread
200 ml/7 fl oz *Greek-style Yogurt* with
2 tsp honey
1 orange

LUNCH
50 g/2 oz bread with low-fat spread
40 g/1½ oz Brie
Carrot, Apple and Beet Salad
1 mango

EVENING
Tomato and Mushroom Risotto
Melon and Strawberry Salad

DAY FIVE

BREAKFAST
As Day One

LUNCH
assortment of crudités and slices of
toast dipped in
Olive Oil and Garlic Sauce
Tuna Pitta Pockets
50 g/2 oz vanilla ice-cream

EVENING
Mushrooms in Garlic Sauce
75 g/3 oz (dry weight) pasta shells,
boiled and served with
Ricotta and Aubergine Sauce
Citrus and Honey Dessert

DAY SIX

BREAKFAST
As Day Two

LUNCH
2 large slices of toast with
Hummus
Large tomato and onion salad with
Oil and Vinegar Dressing
1 banana

EVENING
Tzatziki
Souvlakia
Potato Salad
Green Salad

DAY SEVEN

BREAKFAST
As Day Three

LUNCH
Melted Mozzarella and Tomato
75 g/3 oz crusty bread with
low-fat spread
1 orange

EVENING
75 g/3 oz (dry weight)
tagliatelle, boiled and served with
Walnut Sauce
1 nectarine or peach

TÊTE À TÊTE

A ROMANTIC YET SIMPLE PLAN FOR COUPLES.
ABOUT 2,000 CALORIES PER DAY

Extras per day: 250 ml/8 fl oz skimmed milk, 2 glasses of wine (optional – 3 glasses allowed for men).

DAY ONE
BREAKFAST
$^1/_2$ grapefruit
2 slices of bread or toast from a large loaf with low-fat spread and honey

LUNCH
Tomato Salad
Baked Courgettes
50 g/2 oz roll
140 ml/$^1/_4$ pt Greek-style Yogurt

EVENING
Red Pepper Soup
King Prawn Skewers
50 g/2 oz (dry weight) rice, boiled
sliced cucumber tossed in olive oil and black pepper
Apple and Date Compote

Tomato Salad

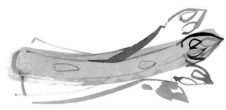

DAY TWO
BREAKFAST
140 ml/$^1/_4$ pt fresh fruit juice of choice
Mixed Fruit Compote
140 ml/$^1/_4$ pt Greek-style yogurt

LUNCH
Tunisian Eggs
75 g/3 oz bread with low-fat spread
1 banana

EVENING
Broad Beans and Mushrooms with 25 g/1 oz slice bread
Lamb Pilaf
Green Salad

DAY THREE
BREAKFAST
1 orange
40 g/1$^1/_2$ oz muesli
140 ml/$^1/_4$ pt Greek-style Yogurt

LUNCH
50 g/2 oz toast with
Tapenade
Stuffed Peppers
Green Salad

EVENING
Baked Sea Bass
Swiss Chard with Pine Nuts
225 g/8 oz baked potato
1 apple

DAY FOUR
BREAKFAST
50 g/2 oz toast with pure fruit spread
50 g/2 oz dried dates or apricots
LUNCH
Aubergine Purée with a little pitta bread
Mussels with Tomato and Basil Sauce
slice of melon

EVENING
Mushrooms in Garlic Sauce
Fillet of Pork Marsala
75 g/3 oz (dry weight) dried noodles, boiled
Green Salad
1 orange

DAY FIVE
BREAKFAST
As Day One

LUNCH
Minestrone Soup with $^1/_2$ portion of *Pesto* stirred into it
1 large bread roll
1 banana

EVENING
Crab and Melon Salad
75 g/3 oz (dry weight) pasta of choice, boiled and served with *Walnut Sauce*
Orange and Fennel Salad

Stuffed Peppers

DAY SIX
BREAKFAST
As Day Two

LUNCH
Bean Dip with a selection of crudités
'The Priest Fainted'
1 mango or 4 apricots

EVENING
Ricotta-stuffed Tomatoes
Squid in Red Wine
Green Salad
Melon and Strawberry Salad

DAY SEVEN
BREAKFAST
As Day Three

LUNCH
Salade Niçoise
50 g/2 oz bread
1 apple

EVENING
Asparagus with Lemon Sauce
Lamb in White Wine
50 g/2 oz (dry weight) rice, boiled
2 apricots or 1 slice of melon

THE FAMILY PLAN

MEALS ALL THE FAMILY WILL ENJOY – BUT WHICH ARE NOT TOO TIME-
CONSUMING FOR THE COOK!
ABOUT 2,000 CALORIES PER DAY

Extras per day: for adults, 250 ml/8 fl oz skimmed milk; for children, 250 ml/8 fl oz whole milk.

DAY ONE
BREAKFAST
Mixed Fruit Compote
140 ml/¼ pt *Greek-style yogurt*
with 1 tsp honey

LUNCH
Minestrone Soup
Pissaladina

EVENING
Sultana-baked Sardines
200 g/7 oz baked potato
Green Salad
Citrus and Honey Dessert

DAY TWO
BREAKFAST
50 g/2 oz bread with low-fat spread
and pure fruit spread
140 ml/¼ pt fresh fruit juice of
choice

LUNCH
Hummus with a selection of crudités
Stuffed Aubergine

EVENING
75 g/3 oz (dry weight) spaghetti,
boiled and served with
Tomato Sauce
Apple and Date Compote
50 g/2 oz vanilla ice-cream

DAY THREE
BREAKFAST
40 g/1½ oz muesli with skimmed
milk
140 g/5 oz fresh fruit of choice
25 g/1 oz bread with low-fat spread
and honey

LUNCH
Yogurt Kebab
½ pitta bread
sliced cucumber

EVENING
Honeyed Chicken
Puréed Potatoes
Swiss Chard with Pine Nuts
1 banana

DAY FOUR
BREAKFAST
200 ml/7 fl oz *Greek-style Yogurt* with
2 tsp honey
140 ml/¼ pt fresh fruit juice of
choice
50 g/2 oz dried apricots

LUNCH
Aubergine Purée with a selection of
crudités and toast
Pasta Crunch
1 orange

EVENING
Rabbit Stiphado
140 g/5 oz carrots
225 g/8 oz baked potato
50 g/2 oz vanilla ice-cream

DAY FIVE
BREAKFAST
As Day One

LUNCH
Lentil Soup
75 g/3 oz chunk of French Bread
1 peach

EVENING
Vegetable Lasagne
Green Salad
Baked Pears
140 ml/¼ pt *Greek-style Yogurt*

DAY SIX
BREAKFAST
As Day Three

LUNCH
Bean Salad
Tuna Pitta Pockets
1 apple

EVENING
Carrot and Potato Purée with a
selection of crudités
Tomato and Mushroom Risotto
½ portion *Mixed Fruit Compote*

DAY SEVEN
BREAKFAST
As Day Four

LUNCH
Tuscan Bean Casserole
50 g/2 oz bread
Tomato Salad

EVENING
Roast Lamb or
Lamb and Apricot Casserole
225 g/8 oz baked potato
French Beans in Orange Sauce

GOURMET DELIGHTS

FOR THOSE WHO ENTERTAIN A GREAT DEAL, OR SIMPLY ENJOY A TOUCH OF
LUXURY AND LOVE TO COOK.
ABOUT 2,000 CALORIES PER DAY

Extras per day: 250 ml/8 fl oz skimmed milk, 3 glasses of wine or champagne.

DAY ONE
BREAKFAST
¹/₂ grapefruit
140 ml/¹/₄ pt *Greek-style Yogurt*
with 140 g/5 oz strawberries and
25 g/1 oz muesli

LUNCH
Roast Yellow Pepper Dip with a
selection of crudités
Crab and Melon Salad
50 g/2 oz French bread with low-fat
spread

EVENING
Ricotta-stuffed Tomatoes
50 g/2 oz French bread dipped in
Olive Oil and Garlic Sauce
Chicken with 30 Cloves of Garlic
Puréed Pumpkin
French Beans in Orange Sauce

DAY TWO
BREAKFAST
Mixed Fruit Compote
25 g/1 oz bread with honey

LUNCH
Mixed Mediterranean Platter
1 mango with
140 ml/¹/₄ pt *Greek-style Yogurt*

EVENING
Swordfish Steaks with Almond Sauce
Spinach with Garlic and Oil
200 g/7 oz boiled potatoes
Peaches in Wine

DAY THREE
BREAKFAST
200 ml/7 fl oz *Greek-style Yogurt*
1 banana
1 orange
1 tsp honey

LUNCH
Red Pepper Soup
Prawn Salad

EVENING
Aubergine Purée with a selection of
crudités
Tzatziki
Souvlakia
pitta bread
Tomato Salad

DAY FOUR
BREAKFAST
50 g/2 oz muesli with skimmed milk
and 100 g/3¹/₂ oz fresh fruit of choice

LUNCH
Asparagus with Lemon Sauce
Scallops with Mushrooms
50 g/2 oz French bread

EVENING
Pork with Oranges
140 g/5 oz broccoli
Carrot and Potato Purée
Banana and Strawberry Sorbets

DAY FIVE
BREAKFAST
As Day One

LUNCH
*Three-nut Salad with Apricots and
Raisins*
50 g/2 oz bread
slice of melon with chopped mint

EVENING
Mushrooms in Garlic Sauce
Paella
Green Salad

DAY SIX
BREAKFAST
As Day Two

LUNCH
Avocado with Lamb's Lettuce
50 g/2 oz bread
1 banana
1 fresh apricot

EVENING
Celery and Artichoke Salad
Spicy Monkfish Kebabs
60 g/2¹/₂ oz (dry weight) rice, boiled
with a little saffron
Citrus and Honey Dessert

DAY SEVEN
BREAKFAST
As Day Three

LUNCH
*Seafood Salad with Three-juice
Dressing*
75 g/3 oz French bread

EVENING
Couscous
Melon and Strawberry Salad

Red Pepper Soup

Spicy Monkfish Kebabs

THE VEGETARIAN PLAN

A HEALTY PLAN FOR THOSE WHO DON'T EAT MEAT, FISH OR POULTRY.
ABOUT 2,000 CALORIES PER DAY

Extras per day: 250 ml/8 fl oz skimmed milk, 2 glasses of wine (optional).

DAY ONE
BREAKFAST
200 ml/7 fl oz *Greek-style Yogurt* with
2 tsp honey
slice of melon
1 orange

LUNCH
Tuscan Bean Casserole
50 g/2 oz bread
50 g/2 oz vanilla ice-cream

EVENING
Aubergine Purée with a selection of
crudités
75 g/3 oz (dry weight) tagliatelle or
pasta spirals, boiled and served with
Walnut Sauce
Baked Pears

DAY TWO
BREAKFAST
Mixed Fruit Compote
140 ml/¼ pt fresh fruit juice of
choice
140 ml/¼ pt *Greek-style Yogurt*

LUNCH
Feta Pitta Pockets
Green Salad

EVENING
Hummus with a selection of crudités
Tunisian Eggs
50 g/2 oz French bread
1 apple
140 ml/¼ pt *Greek-style Yogurt*

DAY THREE
BREAKFAST
50 g/2 oz bread with low-fat spread
and pure fruit spread
1 banana
140 ml/¼ pt fresh fruit juice of
choice

LUNCH
*Broad Bean and Pasta Salad in Orange
Sauce*
Green Salad
50 g/2 oz fresh or dried dates

EVENING
Mushrooms in Garlic Sauce
Stuffed Peppers
Mixed Fruit Compote

DAY FOUR
BREAKFAST
200 ml/7 fl oz *Greek-style Yogurt* with
2 tsp honey
100 g/3½ oz grapes
25 g/1 oz bread with pure fruit spread

LUNCH
*Three-nut Salad with Apricots and
Raisins*
25 g/1 oz bread with low-fat spread

EVENING
75 g/3 oz (dry weight) pasta shells,
boiled and served with
Ricotta and Aubergine Sauce
Green Salad
Citrus and Honey Dessert

DAY FIVE
BREAKFAST
As Day One

LUNCH
Red Pepper Soup
50 g/2 oz Brie with a selection of
crudités and toast

EVENING
Tomato and Mushroom Risotto
vanilla ice-cream
slice of melon or 1 peach

DAY SIX
BREAKFAST
As Day Two

LUNCH
Avocado with Lamb's Lettuce
50 g/2 oz bread
Bean Dip with a selection of crudités

EVENING
Vegetable Lasagne
Green Salad
1 banana
1 orange

DAY SEVEN
BREAKFAST
As Day Three

LUNCH
50 g/2 oz French bread with
Olive Oil and Garlic Sauce
Lentil Soup
2 fresh apricots

EVENING
Broad Beans and Mushrooms
Baked Courgettes
1 orange

LATE PREGNANCY

In the first few months of pregnancy you hardly need to eat any extra calories. However, in the last few months you do need more! This plan provides all the necessary calories plus extra iron and calcium. About 2,300 calories per day

Extras per day: 500 ml/16 fl oz skimmed milk; yogurt and low-fat cheese whenever you like.

DAY ONE
BREAKFAST
40 g/1½ oz muesli with skimmed milk
1 banana
50 g/2 oz bread with low-fat spread and honey

LUNCH
Feta Pitta Pockets
Hummus with a selection of crudités
1 orange

EVENING
Orange and Fennel Salad
6 sardines, grilled
200 g/7 oz boiled potatoes
½ portion *Mixed Fruit Compote*

DAY TWO
BREAKFAST
200 ml/7 fl oz *Greek-style Yogurt* with 2 tsp honey
25 g/1 oz muesli
50 g/2 oz dried apricots
140 ml/¼ pt fresh fruit juice

LUNCH
Pasta Crunch
large slice of melon

EVENING
Roast Lamb
Potato Salad
Pepper and Tomato Stew
Apple and Date Compote

DAY THREE
BREAKFAST
As Day One

LUNCH
Lentil Soup
75 g/3 oz French bread
1 orange

EVENING
One 250 g/9 oz swordfish steak, grilled
Red Pepper and Chilli Sauce
Tabbouleh
Banana and Strawberry Sorbets

DAY FOUR
BREAKFAST
As Day Two

LUNCH
'The Priest Fainted'
50 g/2 oz cottage cheese
50 g/2 oz bread
Green Salad
2 fresh apricots

EVENING
Chicken with Pine Nuts
75 g/3 oz (dry weight) rice, boiled
175 g/6 oz strawberries with
140 ml/¼ pt *Greek-style Yogurt*

DAY FIVE
BREAKFAST
As Day One

LUNCH
Bean Dip with a selection of crudités
Melted Mozzarella and Tomato
75 g/3 oz French bread

EVENING
Ricotta-stuffed Tomatoes
75 g/3 oz (dry weight) pasta, boiled
and served with
Lentil Sauce
Green Salad

DAY SIX
BREAKFAST
As Day Two

LUNCH
Minestrone Soup
Stuffed Peppers
50 g/2 oz bread
1 orange

EVENING
Sardinian Seafood Stew
200 g/7 oz boiled potatoes
Green Salad

DAY SEVEN
BREAKFAST
As Day One

LUNCH
Lentil and Tomato Salad
50 g/2 oz bread
1 banana

EVENING
Celery and Artichoke Salad
Lamb Pilaf
Strawberry and Melon Salad

LOSING WEIGHT
WHILE EATING WELL

Excess weight is a very serious problem in most Western countries and is in itself a health risk. In this chapter we look at just why obesity is

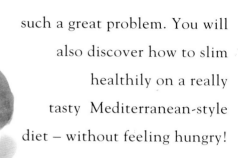

such a great problem. You will also discover how to slim healthily on a really tasty Mediterranean-style diet – without feeling hungry!

It is estimated that at least one-third of the adult population of the Western nations is trying to lose weight at any given time. There are approximately five million *seriously* overweight people in Britain, and in the USA there are more overweight teenagers and young people than ever before.

In other words, despite the availability of thousands of different diets and diet aids, slimming magazines, reduced-calorie foods, and advice from health departments – and despite the fact that most people do realize that being overweight is a real health hazard – obesity is just as much of a problem as ever.

To understand why this is so I think we have to look at the food industry giants who know that 'added value' products – ie, packaged lines – are the ones that make them most profit, not basic fresh foodstuffs. They also finance the multi-billion pound food advertising industry which persuades us at every turn to eat *more*.

The fact is that, although according to Ministry of Agriculture statistics we are eating less fat in its original state – butter, margarine, lard – and less packeted sugar, our overall consumption of fat and sugar has *not* gone down. The fact is that the food manufacturers simply help us to eat what we are not eating in our own cooking by adding more to packet and convenience foods and in 'take-aways'.

Ironically, the people of the more affluent industrialized areas of the Mediterranean are now abandoning their healthy traditional diet in favour of a more Western diet. Imports of butter, white flour and sugar are actually on the increase in this region. Consequently, the populations of these areas are getting fatter and suffering more ill health as a result. This should be a warning to us – and to them!

EATING TO LOSE WEIGHT
You can, in fact eat pasta and oil, rice and bread, and many other good things, including honey and

OPPOSITE: healthy food to enjoy while losing weight

desserts, and still *lose weight*! It is interesting that the people of Britain watching their weight always appear guilty at the thought of tucking into a plate of pasta, or anything with oil on it or in it.

In reality, pasta, oil and most of the rest of the foods of the Mediterranean *are not* fattening. The recipes and foods in this book, wisely used, make a delicious, low-calorie diet for the easiest-ever weight loss..

One of the reasons for its effectiveness is that we virtually eliminate all those pre-packaged convenience foods that almost always contain hidden calories. Instead, you know exactly what you are eating. Another reason is that the Mediterranean diet does not rely on much added fat or sugar, or on a lot of fatty meat and animal produce. So you can easily cope with the calories in the pasta and other carbohydrates and the oil that you will eat. These are the *real* convenience foods – easy to prepare, ready quickly, and healthy!

It is true that olive oil, when compared weight for weight with other foods, is high in calories. However, *you* control the amount you use in recipes and sauces at the table. The taste of olive oil is rich, and you need very little to add superb flavour to any dish. In the Mediterranean, no good chef uses so much olive oil that it is either visible when the dish is served or, with few exceptions, a dominant flavour. Even the high-oil dishes such as *Pesto* and oil-and-vinegar dressing are only intended to coat foods lightly – not to drown them.

Let us compare calorie content in a typical day's eating in Britain and in the Mediterranean.
The day's eating on the left is fairly typical of the kind of menu that you will find throughout Britain and the USA. It is a diet which contains nearly 40% fat, nearly 20% protein and only just over 40% carbohydrate. Although its calorie content is not excessively high, its high-fat, low-carbohydrate content means that it is most certainly not a healthy style of eating.

The Mediterranean-style diet on the right has less than 30% fat, 15% protein and over 55% carbohydrate and the saturated fat content is less than 10%. If you look carefully at the diet on the right, you will probably agree with me that there appears to be *more* to eat, and a better variety of food, than

BRITAIN		MEDITERRANEAN	
Calories		Calories	
BREAKFAST		**BREAKFAST**	
1 boiled egg	80	140 ml/¼ pt yogurt	67
40 g/1½ oz bread	100	1 tsp honey	20
7.5 g/¼ oz butter	53	40 g/1½ oz bread	100
2 tsp marmalade	40	little low-fat spread	20
140 ml/¼ pt orange		2 tsp pure fruit	
juice	50	spread	20
		140 ml/¼ pt orange	
		juice	50
LUNCH		**LUNCH**	
50 g/2 oz bread	140	75 g/3 oz bread	210
15 g/½ oz butter	105	50 g/2 oz Feta cheese	150
50 g/2 oz Cheddar		mixed salad of tomato,	
cheese	240	pepper, onion	40
1 tbsp pickle	30	1 tbsp oil and vinegar	
1 tangerine	25	dressing	80
		1 peach	50
EVENING		**EVENING**	
110 g/4 oz beefburger		*Celery and Artichoke*	
or steak, grilled	235	*Salad*	108
175 g/6 oz medium-		75 g/3 oz (dry weight)	
cut chips	420	pasta (275 g/10 g cooked	
110 g/4 oz peas	60	weight) with	300
75 g/3 oz apple pie	250	*Tomato Sauce*	87
40 g/1½ oz whipping		1 tbsp Parmesan	
cream	150	cheese	20
200 ml/7 fl oz whole		*Melon and Strawberry*	
milk for drinks	126	*Salad*	80
		140 ml/¼ pt yogurt	67
		200 ml/7 fl oz skimmed	
		milk for drinks	70
Total for day	2107	Total for day	1539

in the diet on the left. You would certainly not consider yourself on a low-calorie diet when eating all that lovely-sounding food, would you?

And yet the day's eating on the right contains *600 calories less* than the other. It is a diet on which all men – and many women – would lose weight, albeit slowly. Most men need around 2,700 calories a day, so they'd be cutting calories by 1,000 a day or more, to produce a weekly loss of about 900 g/2 lb.

Most women need around 2,100 calories a day, so they would be eating about 600 calories a day less than they need to maintain weight – enough to produce a 450-675 g/1-1½ lb loss in a week.

However, by making a few more changes to the diet on the right, it is easy to bring its calorie content down even more, to about 1,200 calories, for faster weight loss.

To do this you could easily forgo the low-fat spread at breakfast, have 50 g/2 oz bread and 40 g/1½ oz cheese at lunchtime, have 50 g/2 oz pasta in the evening with a slice of melon rather than the fruit salad, and omit the yogurt. This would save another 300 calories while still leaving you a satisfying diet.

What we are doing to help you lose weight is to reduce the fat content of the diet but keep the carbohydrate content high. It is the carbohydrate foods such as pasta, rice and potatoes that help keep you feeling full, with no dangerous hunger pangs between meals.

To explain this in more detail, here are the percentages of carbohydrate, fat and protein in three different diets.

NORMAL BRITISH DIET
Calories about 2,000
Carbohydrate 45% /900 cal/225 g
Fat 35% /700 cal/77 g
Protein 20% /400 cal/100 g

NORMAL MEDITERRANEAN DIET
Calories about 2,000
Carbohydrate 55% /1,100 cal/275 g
Fat 30% /600 cal/66g
Protein 15% /300 cal/75 g

LOW-CALORIE MEDITERRANEAN DIET
Calories about 1,200
Carbohydrate 65% /780 cal/195 g
Fat 20% /240 cal/270 g
Protein 15% /180 cal/45 g

From these figures you may see that the Mediterranean low-calorie diet gives you 87% of the carbohydrate of the normal British diet, and over 70% of the carbohydrate of the normal Mediterranean diet. This is why it is a good way to slim: it keeps protein

at a safe level of 45 g (the USA recommended daily amount for most women is 44 g) and the fat content of 20% – about 25 g/1 oz a day – allows you room to indulge in olive oil, a little meat, and so on.

As carbohydrate, weight for weight, contain fewer calories by far than fat (carbohydrate has 4 calories per gram and protein has 4 calories per gram, while fat has 9 calories per gram), if you cut animal fat from your diet it is easy to eat sufficient and stay slim.

Even more interestingly the latest research trials in the USA show that a diet high in complex carbohydrates, such as the Mediterranean diet, speeds up the metabolic rate of your body so that there is a further benefit – you are actually burning up the calories you eat more quickly than if you ate, say, a high-fat diet!

So by following the Mediterranean diet, you can lose weight easily. Moreover, because it is so easy to eat less while feeling full, it is highly unlikely that you will ever put weight back on and need to diet again.

Let me summarize the reasons why a Mediterranean diet is the perfect way to slim:
● Meals have real filling power – you never finish a meal feeling hungry.
● Hunger pangs are kept away until the next meal because of the high bulk – plenty of fruit, vegetables and complex carbohydrates.
● The diet is tasty and therefore taste-buds are always satisfied – ordinary diet food seems worlds away.
● The dishes are colourful and appealing to the eye – a very important factor for slimmers.
● Motivation to stay with your diet is high because there is *no deprivation* factor involved.

THE PLANS
The low-calorie plans at the end of this chapter can help everyone to lose weight. I have devised nine different plans so that you may choose whichever one best suits your tastes and your lifestyle. Most supply around 1,200 calories a day, which will achieve a weight loss of about 900 g/2 lb per week for women. Men and teenagers could add extra calories to the diet in the form of extra carbohydrates up to 1,500 a day and still lose weight.

I would not advise you to slim on much fewer calories a day than the levels I have set out. Reducing your food intake too low often results in strong feelings of hunger and deprivation which for most people, sooner or later, end in breaking the diet.

You can swop round the lunch and evening meal in the plans if you prefer – and you can also switch from one plan to another, week after week, to add interest. However, because the plans are nutritionally balanced, it is best not to swop from day to day.

As with the plans in the last chapter, references to recipes from the book (indicated in italics) obviously refer to single portions (one quarter of the total) and quantities should be adjusted accordingly.

HOW MUCH DO YOU NEED TO LOSE?
Decide how much weight you need to lose with the help of the height/weight chart on page 128. If you are near target-weight but are not happy with your shape, it could be that you need to do some regular exercise to tone your body up.

OTHER TIPS TO HELP YOU SLIM
● When you are full at a meal, stop eating. If there is, say, a fruit dessert left, save it for a snack later. Eat slowly, and concentrate on enjoying each mouthful of your food.
● Don't skip meals when you are dieting – you will only become too hungry and be inclined to over-eat later. If you eat regularly, your blood sugar levels remain constant and this helps you to feel good.
● Take some regular daily exercise. Walking, swimming, cycling and aerobics are all good forms of exercise to help burn off calories. A toning routine will also help to reshape your body and firm you up as you lose weight.

FAST & SIMPLE

QUICK AND EASY-TO-PREPARE MEALS FOR BUSY DIETERS.
ABOUT 1,100 CALORIES PER DAY

Extras per day: 148 ml/¹/₄ pt skimmed milk.

DAY ONE
BREAKFAST
Mixed Fruit Compote
100 ml/3¹/₂ fl oz fresh orange juice

LUNCH
Melted Mozzarella and Tomato
Green Salad
1 peach

EVENING
Souvlakia
Tzatziki
sliced tomato and onion salad,
garnished with parsley

DAY TWO
BREAKFAST
140 ml/¹/₄ pt *Greek-style Yogurt*
with 1 tsp honey and 25 g/1 oz
chopped dried apricots
25 g/1 oz bread with pure fruit spread

LUNCH
Tuna Pitta Pockets
1 orange

EVENING
50 g/2 oz (dry weight) spaghetti,
boiled and served with
Tomato Sauce and 1 tbsp grated
Parmesan cheese
Green Salad

DAY THREE
BREAKFAST
two 25 g/1 oz slices of bread with a
little low-fat spread and pure fruit
spread
¹/₂ grapefruit

LUNCH
1 chicken portion, sprinkled with
rosemary and thyme and grilled
Orange and Fennel Salad

EVENING
Baked Courgettes
Tomato Salad
50 g/2 oz bread

Fresh Fruit Platter.

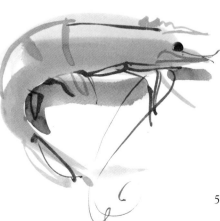

DAY FOUR
BREAKFAST
Fresh fruit platter: 250 g/9 oz
fruit of choice
50 g/2 oz low-fat soft cheese

LUNCH
Pasta Crunch
sliced cucumber and onion salad

EVENING
Spicy Monkfish Kebabs
50 g/2 oz (dry weight) rice, boiled
Green Salad

DAY FIVE
BREAKFAST
As Day One

LUNCH
Bean Dip with a selection of crudités
25 g/1 oz bread
25 g/1 oz Brie
1 apple

EVENING
Pork with Oranges
140 g/5 oz carrots and 140 g/5 oz
broccoli, lightly cooked
Melon and Strawberry Salad

DAY SIX
BREAKFAST
As Day Two

LUNCH
Crab and Melon Salad
50 g/2 oz bread with a little low-fat
spread

EVENING
75 g/3 oz (dry weight)
fettuccine, boiled and served with
Mushroom Sauce
Green Salad
Citrus and Honey Dessert

DAY SEVEN
BREAKFAST
As Day Three

LUNCH
Feta Pitta Pockets
140 ml/¹/₄ pt *Greek-style Yogurt*
1 orange

EVENING
Prawns Provençal
50 g/2 oz (dry weight) rice, boiled
Green Salad
Peaches in Wine

THE FAMILY DIET

LOSE WEIGHT WITH MEALS WHICH ALL THE FAMILY WILL ENJOY. THOSE WHO ARE
NOT DIETING CAN EAT MORE BREAD, POTATOES, PASTA OR RICE THAN THE
QUANTITIES GIVEN.
ABOUT 1,200 CALORIES PER DAY

Extras per day: 250 ml/8 fl oz skimmed milk.

DAY ONE
BREAKFAST
140 ml/¼ pt fresh fruit juice of
choice
½ portion *Mixed Fruit Compote*
140 ml/¼ pt *Greek-style Yogurt*

LUNCH
Salade Niçoise
100 g/3½ oz grapes or strawberries

EVENING
Rabbit Stiphado
175 g/6 oz potatoes, boiled or baked
140 g/4 oz green vegetables of
choice, lightly cooked

DAY TWO
BREAKFAST
50 g/2 oz bread with a little low-fat
spread and honey
1 orange

LUNCH
Lentil and Tomato Soup
lettuce and cucumber

EVENING
Spicy Monkfish Kebabs
40 g/1½ oz rice (dry weight), boiled

DAY THREE
BREAKFAST
40 g/1½ oz muesli
with 140 ml/¼ pt skimmed milk
1 orange

LUNCH
'The Priest Fainted'
25 g/1 oz bread
50 g/2 oz vanilla ice-cream

EVENING
Lamb and Apricot Casserole
50 g/2 oz (cooked weight) boiled
potatoes or rice
lettuce garnish

DAY FOUR
BREAKFAST
As Day one

LUNCH
Mixed Mediterranean Platter
2 fresh apricots

EVENING
Vegetable Lasagne
Green Salad
Melon and Strawberry Salad

DAY FIVE
BREAKFAST
As Day Two

LUNCH
Minestrone Soup
40 g/1½ oz bread
1 apple

EVENING
250 g/9 oz white fish of choice,
grilled
Tomato Sauce
140 g/5 oz boiled potatoes
French Beans in Orange Sauce

DAY SIX
BREAKFAST
As Day Three

LUNCH
Feta Pitta Pockets

EVENING
75 g/3 oz (dry weight) pasta of
choice, boiled and served with
Mushroom Sauce
Apple and Date Compote

DAY SEVEN
BREAKFAST
As Day One

LUNCH
Baked Courgettes
40 g/1½ oz bread
140 g/5 oz soft fruit of choice with
a little *Greek-style Yogurt*
EVENING
Rice with Peppers and Pork
Green Salad
1 apple

Feta Pitta Pockets

THE ROMANTIC DIET

SERVE VERY SPECIAL MEALS FOR YOU AND YOUR PARTNER - WITHOUT YOUR
OTHER HALF NECESSARILY EVEN KNOWING YOU ARE BOTH DIETING!
ABOUT 1,200 CALORIES PER DAY

Extras per day: 250 ml/8 fl oz skimmed milk, 1 glass of dry wine. Partners may add extra
rice, potatoes, pasta or bread to each meal if they are not dieting.

DAY ONE
BREAKFAST
^{1}/$_2$ grapefruit or
100 ml/3^1/$_2$ fl oz tomato juice
140 ml/^{1}/$_4$ pt *Greek-style Yogurt*
25 g/1 oz bread with a little low-fat
spread and 2 tsp honey or pure fruit
spread

LUNCH
*Three-nut Salad with Apricots
and Raisins*

EVENING
*Celery and Artichoke Salad
Mussels with Tomato and Basil Sauce*
25 g/1 oz bread
Peaches in Wine

DAY TWO
BREAKFAST
As Day One

LUNCH
Tapenade with 40 g/1^1/$_2$ oz toast
Crab and Melon Salad

EVENING
*Honeyed Chicken
Pumpkin Purée*
100 g/3^1/$_2$ oz broccoli, lightly cooked

DAY THREE
BREAKFAST
As Day One

LUNCH
*Broad Bean and Pasta Salad in
Orange Sauce*
25 g/1 oz bread

EVENING
*Squid in Red Wine
Green Salad
Melon and Strawberry Salad*

DAY FOUR
BREAKFAST
As Day One

LUNCH
Melted Mozzarella and Tomato
40 g/1^1/$_2$ oz bread

EVENING
50 g/2 oz (dry weight) pasta of
choice, boiled and served with
*Ricotta and Aubergine Sauce
Green Salad*

DAY FIVE
BREAKFAST
As Day One

LUNCH
Avocado with Lamb's Lettuce
3 fresh apricots

EVENING
*Red Pepper Soup
Lamb in White Wine*
25 g/1 oz (dry weight) rice, boiled

DAY SIX
BREAKFAST
As Day One

LUNCH
*Seafood Salad with Three-juice
Dressing*
25 g/1 oz bread

EVENING
Pork with Oranges
40 g/1^1/$_2$ oz (dry weight) noodles,
boiled
100 g/3^1/$_2$ oz French beans, lightly
cooked

DAY SEVEN
BREAKFAST
As Day One

LUNCH
Tunisian Eggs
40 g/1^1/$_2$ oz bread
100 g/3^1/$_2$ oz strawberries

EVENING
Prawns Provençal
50 g/2 oz (dry weight) rice, boiled
Green Salad

Leafy Green Salad

THE DEMI-VEGETARIAN DIET

A SLIMMING PLAN FOR ALL THOSE WHO DON'T EAT RED MEAT BUT
OCCASIONALLY ENJOY MEALS WHICH INCLUDE FISH OR POULTRY.
ABOUT 1,200 CALORIES PER DAY

Extras per day: 275 ml/9 fl oz skimmed milk.

King Prawn Skewers

DAY ONE
BREAKFAST
¹/₂ portion *Mixed Fruit Compote*
140 ml/¹/₄ pt *Greek-style Yogurt*

LUNCH
Hummus with 50 g/2 oz toast
slice of melon or 1 orange

EVENING
Tomato and Mushroom Risotto
lettuce garnish
1 banana

DAY TWO
BREAKFAST
¹/₂ grapefruit
25 g/1 oz muesli with 140 ml/¹/₄ pt
skimmed milk

LUNCH
Tuna Pitta Pockets
40 g/1¹/₂ oz dried apricots

EVENING
Sultana-baked Sardines
Green Salad
1 apple

DAY THREE
BREAKFAST
1 orange
40 g/1¹/₂ oz bread with a little
low-fat spread and 2 tsp honey

LUNCH
Ratatouille with 1 poached egg
on top
40 g/1¹/₂ oz bread
4 fresh or dried dates

EVENING
75 g/3 oz (dry weight)
spaghetti, boiled and served with
Pesto
lettuce side salad

DAY FOUR
BREAKFAST
As Day One

LUNCH
'The Priest Fainted'
40 g/1¹/₂ oz bread
1 peach or nectarine

EVENING
King Prawn Skewers
50 g/2 oz (dry weight) rice,
boiled
sliced cucumber
Citrus and Honey Dessert

DAY FIVE
BREAKFAST
As Day Two

LUNCH
Tuscan Bean Casserole
25 g/1 oz bread
lettuce side salad

EVENING
Baked Courgettes
Tomato Salad
50 g/2 oz bread
Apple and Date Compote

DAY SIX
BREAKFAST
As Day Three

LUNCH
Salade Niçoise
1 apricot

EVENING
Bean Dip with a selection of crudités
Pasta Crunch

DAY SEVEN
BREAKFAST
As Day One

LUNCH
Aubergine Purée with a selection of
crudités
50 g/2 oz feta cheese
40 g/1¹/₂ oz bread
2 or 3 sticks of celery

EVENING
Mushrooms in Garlic Sauce
1 red mullet, grilled or baked
Tabbouleh
Tomato Salad

THE VEGETARIAN DIET

THIS PLAN CONTAINS NO MEAT, POULTRY, FISH OR EGGS. THERE ARE SMALL
AMOUNTS OF MILK AND CHEESE IN SOME RECIPES, BUT VEGANS CAN REPLACE
THESE WITH SOYA MILK AND TOFU.
ABOUT 1,200 CALORIES PER DAY

Extras per day: 250 ml/8 fl oz skimmed milk or soya milk.

DAY ONE
BREAKFAST
1/2 portion *Mixed Fruit Compote*
100 ml/3 1/2 fl oz skimmed milk or
soya milk
1/2 grapefruit

LUNCH
Stuffed Peppers
Green Salad

EVENING
75 g/3 oz (dry weight) pasta of
choice, boiled and served with
Walnut Sauce

DAY TWO
BREAKFAST
1/2 grapefruit
140 ml/1/4 pt *Greek-style Yogurt*
topped with 40 g/1 1/2 oz dried fruit of
choice and 25 g/1 oz muesli

LUNCH
Lentil Soup
20 g/3/4 oz bread

EVENING
Mushrooms in Garlic Sauce
Pissaladina
Melon and Strawberry Salad

DAY THREE
BREAKFAST
40 g/1 1/2 oz bread with a little low-fat
spread and 2 tsp honey
1 orange

LUNCH
Tuscan Bean Casserole
Green Salad

EVENING
Tzatziki with a selection of crudités
Vegetable Lasagne
1 banana

Melon & Strawberry Salad

DAY FOUR
BREAKFAST
25 g/1 oz shelled nuts, such as
almonds
1 peach, nectarine or orange

LUNCH
Tapenade with 40 g/1 1/2 oz toast
Broad Beans and Mushrooms
lettuce garnish

EVENING
Orange and Fennel Salad
Lentil and Tomato Soup

DAY FIVE
BREAKFAST
As Day One

LUNCH
Red Pepper Soup
40 g/1 1/2 oz bread
Ricotta-stuffed Tomatoes

EVENING
Three-nut Salad with Apricots
and Raisins
Tabbouleh

DAY SIX
BREAKFAST
As Day Two

LUNCH
Carrot, Apple and Beet Salad
Broad Bean and Pasta Salad in
Orange Sauce

EVENING
Tomato and Mushroom Risotto
Peaches in Wine

DAY SEVEN
BREAKFAST
As Day Three

LUNCH
Hummus with 1 pitta bread and a
selection of crudités
1 apple

EVENING
75 g/3 oz (dry weight) pasta of
choice, served with
Tomato Sauce
Baked Pears

THE WEEKEND RELAXER

THIS DIET PLAN CUTS THE CALORIES MOSTLY DURING THE BUSY WORKING WEEK,
BUT ALLOWS YOU TO ENJOY YOURSELF AND EAT A LITTLE MORE AT WEEKENDS.
ABOUT 1,000 CALORIES PER WEEKDAY (DAYS 1 TO 5)
ABOUT 1,700 CALORIES PER DAY AT THE WEEKEND (DAYS 6 & 7)

Extras per day: 250 ml/8 fl oz skimmed milk, 2 glasses medium or dry wine each day
at the weekend.

DAY ONE
BREAKFAST
200 ml/7 fl oz *Greek-style Yogurt*
2 pieces of fresh fruit of choice, such
as apple, pear, peach, nectarine,
orange, grapefruit or 140 g/5 oz soft
fruit

LUNCH
50 g/2 oz feta cheese crumbled on
Tomato Salad
1 pitta bread

EVENING
Rice with Peppers and Pork
lettuce garnish

DAY TWO
BREAKFAST
As Day One

LUNCH
4 fresh sardines, grilled
40 g/1¹/₂ oz bread
cucumber slices

EVENING
75 g/3 oz (dry weight) pasta of
choice, boiled and served with
Mushroom Sauce
lettuce garnish

DAY THREE
BREAKFAST
As Day One

LUNCH
Ricotta-stuffed Tomatoes
40 g/1¹/₂ oz bread

EVENING
Scallops with Mushrooms
40 g/1¹/₂ oz (dry weight) rice, boiled
watercress and lettuce garnish

DAY FOUR
BREAKFAST
As Day One

LUNCH
Melted Mozzarella and Tomato
40 g/1¹/₂ oz bread

EVENING
Pasta Crunch
cucumber slices

DAY FIVE
BREAKFAST
As Day One

LUNCH
Tuna Pitta Pockets
1 fresh apricot

EVENING
Mixed Mediterranean Platter
1 banana

DAY SIX
BREAKFAST
As Day One *plus*
25 g/1 oz bread with a little low-fat
spread and pure fruit spread or honey

LUNCH
Asparagus with Lemon Sauce
Bean Salad
Green Salad

EVENING
slice of melon
Paella
Peaches in Wine

DAY SEVEN
BREAKFAST
As Day Six

LUNCH
Hummus with a selection of
crudités
Stuffed Peppers

EVENING
Red Pepper Soup
Lamb Pilaf
Citrus and Honey Dessert

Ricotta Stuffed Tomatoes

THE POST-PREGNANCY DIET

THIS PLAN IS SPECIFICALLY DEVISED FOR NURSING MOTHERS WHO WOULD LIKE TO
LOSE WEIGHT STEADILY. THOSE MOTHERS WHO ARE NOT BREASTFEEDING MAY
FOLLOW THE OTHER LOW-CALORIE PLANS.
ABOUT 1,700 CALORIES PER DAY

Extras per day: 500 ml/16 fl oz skimmed milk, 1 banana and plenty of low-calorie fluids,
especially water.

DAY ONE
BREAKFAST
200 ml/7 fl oz fresh fruit juice of
choice
40 g/1¹/₂ oz muesli with
140 ml/¹/₄ pt *Greek-style Yogurt*

LUNCH
Bean Dip with a selection of crudités
Melted Mozzarella and Tomato
25 g/1 oz bread

EVENING
Lamb Pilaf
Green Salad

DAY TWO
BREAKFAST
Mixed Fruit Compote with
4 tbsp *Greek-style Yogurt*

LUNCH
Salade Niçoise
40 g/1¹/₂ oz bread
1 orange

EVENING
75 g/3 oz (dry weight) pasta of
choice, boiled and served with
Lentil Sauce
Green Salad

DAY THREE
BREAKFAST
40 g/1¹/₂ oz bread with a little low-fat
spread and pure fruit spread or honey
140 ml/¹/₄ pt *Greek-style Yogurt*

LUNCH
slice of melon
50 g/2 oz feta cheese
Carrot, Apple and Beet Salad
75 g/3 oz bread

EVENING
Fillet of Pork Marsala
50 g/2 oz (dry weight) dried noodles,
boiled
100 g/3¹/₂ oz broccoli, lightly cooked

Salade Niçoise

DAY FOUR
BREAKFAST
As Day One

LUNCH
Tunisian Eggs
50 g/2 oz bread
1 banana

EVENING
Baked Sea Bass
140 g/5 oz boiled potatoes
Spinach with Garlic and Oil

DAY FIVE
BREAKFAST
As Day Two

LUNCH
5 sardines, pan-fried in a little olive
oil
50 g/2 oz bread
Green Salad

EVENING
Vegetable Lasagne
Baked Pears

DAY SIX
BREAKFAST
As Day Three

LUNCH
Tuscan Bean Casserole with 2 tbsp
grated Parmesan cheese

EVENING
Honeyed Chicken
Carrot and Potato Purée
100 g/3¹/₂ oz French beans, lightly
cooked

DAY SEVEN
BREAKFAST
As Day One

LUNCH
Lentil Soup
50 g/2 oz bread
1 orange

EVENING
Beef Stiphado
225 g/8 oz baked potato
200 g/7 oz cabbage or other green
vegetable, lightly cooked

THE WINTER DIET

THIS PLAN PROVIDES EXTRA CALORIES TO ALLOW YOU TO DIET THROUGH THE
WINTER MONTHS AND ALSO INCLUDES PLENTY OF WARMING DISHES TO KEEP THE
COLD AT BAY.

ABOUT 1,300 CALORIES PER DAY

Extras: 250 ml/8 fl oz skimmed milk.

DAY ONE

BREAKFAST
50 g/2 oz toast with a little low-fat
spread and honey
140 ml/¼ pt fresh fruit juice of
choice

LUNCH
Lentil Soup
25 g/1 oz bread
1 orange

EVENING
Yogurt Kebab
1 satsuma

DAY TWO

BREAKFAST
½ portion *Mixed Fruit Compote*
140 ml/¼ pt hot skimmed milk
140 ml/¼ pt fresh fruit juice of
choice

LUNCH
Stuffed Aubergines
5 fresh dates or 1 apple

EVENING
Sardinian Seafood Stew
20 g/¾ oz bread

DAY THREE

BREAKFAST
25 g/1 oz porridge oats, cooked
with skimmed milk and mixed with
25 g/1 oz chopped dried fruit of
choice
140 ml/¼ pt fresh fruit juice of
choice

LUNCH
Tuscan Bean Casserole
25 g/1 oz bread
1 orange

EVENING
Rice with Peppers and Pork
Apple and Date Compote

DAY FOUR

BREAKFAST
As Day One

LUNCH
Pissaladina

EVENING
Beef Stiphado
200 g/7 oz baked potato
140 g/4 oz cabbage or other greens,
lightly cooked

DAY FIVE

BREAKFAST
As Day Two

LUNCH
Tunisian Eggs
50 g/2 oz bread
1 banana

EVENING
75 g/3 oz (dry weight) spaghetti,
boiled and served with
Lentil Sauce

DAY SIX

BREAKFAST
As Day Three

LUNCH
Minestrone Soup
50 g/2 oz bread
1 orange

EVENING
Lamb and Apricot Casserole
25 g/1 oz (dry weight) rice, boiled

DAY SEVEN

BREAKFAST
As Day One

LUNCH
½ portion *Hummus* with a selection
of crudités
4 sardines, grilled
40 g/1½ oz bread

EVENING
Chicken with 30 Cloves of Garlic
Carrot and Potato Purée
140 g/4 oz cabbage or other
greens, lightly cooked

Stuffed Aubergines

Grilled Sardines

44

THE SUMMER SIZZLER

WITH LITTLE COOKING AND PLENTY OF APPEALING SALADS THIS DIET IS IDEAL
FOR THOSE SUMMER MONTHS WHEN THE HEAT IS ON.
ABOUT 1,200 CALORIES PER DAY

Extras per day: 250 ml/8 fl oz skimmed milk, one glass of chilled white wine or
champagne.

DAY THREE
BREAKFAST
As Day One

LUNCH
Melted Mozzarella and Tomato
40 g/1¹/₂ oz bread
1 apple

EVENING
Mushrooms in Garlic Sauce
Bean Salad
Green Salad
140 g/4 oz strawberries with 2 tbsp
Greek-style Yogurt and 1 tsp sugar

DAY FOUR
BREAKFAST
As Day One

LUNCH
Broad Bean and Pasta Salad in Orange
Sauce
1 nectarine

EVENING
Three-nut Salad with Apricots and
Raisins
Banana and Strawberry Sorbets

DAY FIVE
BREAKFAST
As Day One

LUNCH
Tuna Pitta Pockets
100 g/3¹/₂ oz grapes or strawberries

EVENING
Mixed Mediterranean Platter
Peaches in Wine

DAY SIX
BREAKFAST
As Day One

LUNCH
Seafood Salad with Three-juice
Dressing
1 peach

EVENING
60 g/2¹/₂ oz (dry weight) pasta of
choice, boiled and served with
Pesto
lettuce side salad

DAY SEVEN
BREAKFAST
As Day One

LUNCH
Tabbouleh
50 g/2 oz cooked chicken
1 banana

EVENING
Prawn Salad

DAY ONE
BREAKFAST
200 ml/7 fl oz *Greek-style Yogurt*
2 portions of fresh fruit from the
following: 1 nectarine, 1 peach, 2
plums, 1 mango, 1 orange,
1 grapefruit, 1 large slice of melon,
100 g/3¹/₂ oz cherries, strawberries or
raspberries

LUNCH
Feta Pitta Pockets

EVENING
Salade Niçoise
40 g/1¹/₂ oz bread
Melon and Strawberry Salad

DAY TWO
BREAKFAST
As Day One

LUNCH
Tapenade with a selection of crudités
Crab and Melon Salad

EVENING
Avocado with Lamb's Lettuce
40 g/1¹/₂ oz bread
Citrus and Honey Dessert

Broad Bean & Pasta Salad

THE MEDITERRANEAN KITCHEN

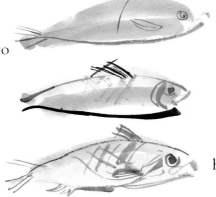

Changing from the Western to the Mediterranean style of eating will involve some quite different patterns of shopping and stocking the store-cupboard. This chapter takes a good look at some of the most important Mediterranean ingredients and has advice on buying and storage.

If you are changing to a Mediterranean diet, you will need to do a certain amount of rethinking and restocking in the larder and kitchen. Foods that have formed a small part of your meals will now form a large part; and foods previously much used will now be relegated to an occasional role.

In this chapter I will take you through the contents of your new storecupboard and refrigerator and give a guide to what ingredients you will need as permanent stock, where to buy them and which varieties to buy, where appropriate. Despite its great reliance on fresh produce, having a good, varied store is one of the most important parts of the Mediterranean kitchen. Dried foods, preserved foods and even cans are traditionally a big part of the Mediterranean cook's kitchen and staples are always readily available to make up a quick meal, not just when fresh produce is in short supply but all year round as well.

A few years ago it was hard to find all the necessary ingredients for Mediterranean cooking in Britain, unless you lived, for example, within shopping distance of London's Soho, which has always had a myriad of ethnic food shops tucked away down its side streets. Now it becomes easier every year to find what you want; if the supermarket doesn't have it, the local delicatessen or health-food shop certainly will. Perhaps the hardest thing to find is a good choice of Mediterranean fish and shellfish. However, acceptable alternatives can usually be found and substituted.

Necessary kitchen utensils will probably not vary much from those you have in your home already. Though you can invest in authentic pasta pans and couscousières, etc, if you wish to.

THE STORECUPBOARD
OLIVE OIL is the perfect oil for all cooking, salad and dressing needs as there are so many different varieties each with their own particular character.

OPPOSITE: raspberries in wine vinegar and extra virgin olive oil

It may be heated safely to very high temperatures and, in tests, food fried in olive oil absorbs at least 12% less oil than food fried in other oils or fats. You therefore get a lighter finished dish, and of course fewer calories.

Olive oils from Spain, Italy and Greece are widely available in Britain. Italian olive oil is considered the best by many. Of course, the Greeks, Spanish and other olive oil producers would *not* agree! Within each country there are also various distinctive regional varieties of oils. For instance, within Italy, some connoisseurs prefer the oil of Tuscany; while others say that Liguria oil is superior. However, like a wine buff, the olive oil connoisseur will take years to learn his or her preferences and know the oils well. If you are a beginner, it is important to know the different qualities of oil.

Virgin olive oil comes from the first pressing of the olives. You may also see the words 'first pressing' or 'cold pressed' on the label. Some labels will state that the oil is *extra virgin* – this means that it has no more than 1% acidity, whereas 'virgin' oil may have up to 3.3% acidity. If any olive oil isn't virgin, it will simply be labelled *pure olive oil* and will come from a later pressing of the olives. There may be several pressings and usually the least expensive olive oils will be from the last pressings.

Although the colour and flavour of olive oils varies very much from country to country , olive to olive, and year to year, broadly, the virgin oils are usually a more distinctive greener, and/or richer golden colour, with a stronger distinctive, richer and more fruity taste. They are ideal for salad dressings and for using neat on pasta, bread etc.

The oil of the later pressings will usually be a lighter colour: pale yellow or gold, with a lighter taste. These oils are good for frying and sautéing and for casseroles, etc. If you find the taste of virgin oil *too* strong – which some people do – you may actually prefer to use a 'pure olive oil' for all purposes.

I suggest that to begin with, you buy one virgin or extra virgin oil and one later pressing oil – as you use up each bottle you can try a different brand next time, until you discover the ones you prefer. For this reason it is best at first to buy olive oil in smaller bottles rather, say, than the 5–litre cans you can find in some delicatessens!

Most supermarkets now stock at least a few varieties of olive oil. You may find more choice in any good delicatessen, or perhaps a health-food shop. Alternatively, if you live in a city, the food halls of department stores usually have a good range, and some wine shops also now stock quality olive oils.

Keep your olive oil in a cool, dark place and it will last for a long time – not that it needs to!

WINE VINEGAR is used by Mediterranean cooks much as the British use malt vinegar. So abandon your malt and stock up with red and white wine vinegar, either plain or flavoured with herbs for variety. I prefer red wine vinegar for its richer colour and flavour, but white wine vinegar is perfectly suitable both for cooking and for dressings, especially with fish and poultry dishes. An easy way to impart garlic flavour to salad is to steep crushed cloves in the vinegar before making your dressing.

PASTA may be made at home if you have a lot of spare time and, preferably, a pasta cutting machine. Alternatively, you can do what most people do and buy dried pasta, which I find perfectly acceptable and many people actually prefer. Buy only 100% durum wheat pasta. Don't buy any other kind as it won't give you that nice firm, unsticky, 'al dente' texture, and will all too often cook to a mush. If you can't find the words '100% durum wheat' on the label of pasta, just don't buy it. Obviously, pasta made in Italy is the best.

Wholewheat pasta contains a little more fibre than durum wheat pasta, but I find the texture and taste poor in comparison. Ordinary durum wheat pasta contains wheatgerm, which is a plus. If you prefer wholewheat, it can be used in any of the recipes in this book, but it will need longer cooking.

Ready-made fresh pasta is available in the chilled cabinets at many delicatessens and supermarkets. The quality of such pasta varies tremendously. If you find a good source, don't forget it only needs a few minutes' cooking.

There are many different shapes of pasta. In Italy you will find at least 100 and probably more. In Britain there is a reasonable choice at supermarkets and if you have an Italian delicatessen near you, the choice will be great.

The Italians select their pasta shapes according to what will 'marry' best with the sauce. For instance, long spaghetti is best served with a sauce which contains no large pieces and is fairly liquid so that it will cling to the pasta – tomato sauce or plain olive oil and Parmesan are ideal. Shells and short shapes suit heavier sauces with larger chunks of food in it, and hollow pasta likes a creamy sauce that will run inside it as well as cling to it.

Apart from plain pasta you can also buy pasta verdi, which is coloured green with spinach, and red pasta made with tomato. These add a little extra flavour, but the addition of colour to the plate is perhaps the main reason that these pastas are used. They are also pretty in salads, and if your sauce is a neutral colour, like walnut or mushroom, a green or red pasta will look more appetizing.

Experiment with your own pasta shapes, colours and combinations. Whatever you do, learn to cook pasta well. It hates to be overcooked and/or kept hanging around as it loses heat very quickly.

Boil plenty of lightly salted water in a large pan, add a dash of olive oil to prevent the pasta sticking together. Test a small piece of pasta a minute before the end of cooking time stated on the packet. When 'al dente' – ie tender but still firm to the bite – remove the pasta from the heat immediately, drain and serve promptly.

RICE AND GRAINS are staples of the region. Rice is the principal grain used throughout the Mediter-ranean, apart from North Africa where couscous is favoured. The Mediterraneans frequently use *short-grain rice* for savoury dishes but, apart from the special short-grain *Arborio* or *risotto rice* which may be found in Britain, you will probably have to settle for *patna rice* in all recipes where rice is mentioned. You can use patna or risotto rice for paella, but I prefer *long-grain rice* and even sometimes use the Indian *basmati rice* for its fuller flavour.

The Mediterraneans don't make much use of *brown rice*, but you can use it in salad recipes and side dishes if you prefer. It does not work well in risottos, pilafs or paellas, as it tends to remain firm to the bite and doesn't absorb the liquids of the dish as it should.

Couscous is the grain of Morocco and Tunisia. It is made from hard wheat, and you can generally buy it in health-food shops and delicatessens. It is sim-ply soaked to swell it up and then steamed over the stew with which it is to be served. A little goes a long way, as it swells greatly during cooking.

Bulgar is an Eastern Mediterranean pre-cooked cracked wheat. It is first soaked for a few minutes and then used in salads such as *Tabbouleh*. It too is available from health-food shops and delicatessens.

PULSES, such as dried beans, peas and lentils are widely used throughout the Mediterranean. They can be put into salads and are frequently used as the bases for soups and stews. They may also be used to make sauces and dips, or they can be served on their own as a hot side dish, perhaps flavoured with herbs or tomatoes.

Although you can buy pulses in small boxes or packs from the supermarket, which will probably have a small selection of the most popular types, I prefer to go the delicatessen or health-food shop for mine. This is not only because the selection will be larger, but because you can buy in bulk. As pulses keep for a long time stored in dry conditions, this makes a great deal of sense.

It is also worth buying some canned beans. As they are pre-cooked, if you forget to soak your dried beans you have a quick standby. Also, I find canned chickpeas, for instance, much nicer than dried ones when making *Hummus*, and canned red kidney beans are certainly as nice as the dried ones.

Dried beans, especially chickpeas and kidney beans, need to be soaked for several hours or over-night. The soaking water is then discarded and the beans boiled rapidly in fresh water for 10 minutes to remove toxins. The beans are then simmered for an hour or two until tender. Do *not* add salt to pulses until they are cooked as it makes them tough.

The best lentils to buy are the small brown ones (my favourites) or the green ones, in preference to the orange ones which have less flavour. Lentils do not need any pre-soaking.

Not all beans taste the same. The following are some the Mediterraneans enjoy regularly:

Borlotti: a pale, pinky-brown Italian bean used in salads and casseroles.

Broad beans: these are brown if they still have their skins and white if the skin has been removed; they make good salads and soups.

OVERLEAF: the Mediterranean larder

Cannellini: creamy haricot-type bean used in classic Italian dishes.

Chickpeas: these hard round 'peas' are popular in North Africa and the Eastern Mediterranean.

Flageolet: pretty pale-green variety of haricot.

Haricot: the most common Mediterranean bean, small and white, used in casseroles and very good with lamb and pork dishes.

Kidney beans: these go into Italian soups and salads, and are included in casseroles throughout the Mediterranean.

DRIED FRUITS, such as apricots, peaches, figs, plums (prunes), dates, and grapes (sultanas and raisins) may all be found in the Mediterranean and they are used in cooking all the time – in hot fruit dishes, in savoury dishes and salads, with yogurt, or just as a snack on their own. Here you can buy small packs of dried fruit at the supermarket, but you may cut costs and find more variety at the health-food shop. Remember to store dried fruit in airtight containers.

NUTS AND SEEDS are much favoured in Mediterranean cooking. For value, these are best bought loose from the health-food shop rather than in the tiny packets you normally get in the supermarkets. However, don't buy too many nuts at once as they do lose flavour and become dry if kept more than a few weeks, shelled or unshelled.

Almonds: a particular favourite in Spain where they are used in a variety of dishes, whole, toasted or ground.

Pine nuts: are a classic ingredient of Mediterranean cooking. They have a distinctive taste which no other nut can match, and a soft, melting texture. They are available in Britain but are not easy to obtain everywhere as some shopkeepers consider them too expensive to stock. However, a few of these nuts go a long way, and I have managed to persuade my local delicatessen owner to order some especially for me. If a minimum order is too much for you, arrange to split it amongst friends.

Walnuts: make fabulous sauces and are one of my favourite salad additions. For sauces you can buy the less costly walnut pieces rather than the halves.

Sesame seeds: are widely used sprinkled on vegetables or sweet dishes, or ground into the famous tahini paste of Greece and the Lebanon.

Sunflower seeds: make a nutritious snack or addition to a breakfast muesli.

TINS AND JARS are very useful, even if fresh or dried natural ingredients are so important in Mediterranean cooking. There are a few cans, jars or tubes that I advise you to stock up your larder with, without any need to feel that you are in any way letting the side down!

Fish: you will be hard-pressed to find fresh or frozen anchovies in this country and it is also not easy to find fresh or frozen tuna, so I suggest you stock up with some little cans of both. Buy tuna in oil rather than tuna in brine which, although it contains fewer calories, has probably lost most of its Omega-3 oils. If you drain the fish well, the calorie count won't actually be much higher.

Tomatoes: you will find canned tomatoes mentioned in many of the recipes in this book. This is because Italian plum tomatoes are full of flavour and very versatile and, unless you can get such very ripe, very tasty, true Mediterranean tomatoes, I think canned tomatoes work better. Under-ripe, under-tasty, small British tomatoes are no substitute. Also buy tomato paste, preferably the kind with no added salt.

Tahini: buy a jar of tahini, preferably the light tahini. You could possibly make your own, but I am sure you could make it no better.

Honey: a jar of runny Greek honey on your shelf is a must!

Olives: you can buy olives either black or green, stoned or unstoned, stuffed or plain, packed in jars, cans or vacuum-sealed. My own preference is for black stoned olives, either in jars or vacuum packs. Go for the largest, plumpest olives you can find, and rinse them before you use them to take away some of the saltiness. Serve olives with aperitifs, as part of a selection of mezes or tapas or on their own. You can also use them as a garnish on salads.

HERBS are the heart of Mediterranean cooking. It is a pity for us that we can't walk to a nearby hillside and pick wild thyme, rosemary, parsley, basil or coriander as many Mediterraneans still can. Although dried herbs bought from the supermarket can be a reasonable substitute, fresh is almost always best. If you have a garden or patio, consider starting a herb plot as most herbs are quite easy to grow and thrive throughout the summer in a sunny spot. Otherwise, some supermarket chains now stock growing herbs for your windowsill, and fresh cut herbs in small packets.

I know dried herbs in glass jars look pretty in the kitchen, but if you do have to buy dried this is absolutely the worst way to store them if you still want them to taste or smell of anything in a week or two. The rule with dried herbs is to buy in small quantities and store them away from heat and light to retain their flavour and aroma.

The following are the most widely used Mediterranean herbs:

Basil: one of Italy's favourites and particularly good with tomatoes. Easy to grow. The dried herb is strong, so use sparingly.

Bay leaves: sweet herb which does dry and keep well. Ideal with lamb and fish and in stews.

Chives: these do not dry well but can easily be grown on a windowsill. Fresh chopped chives are a wonderful garnish for salads and soups.

Coriander leaves: chop them up for salads and leave them whole for garnishes.

Garlic: hardly a herb, in Mediterranean terms, as so much is used. Buy the biggest, firmest bulbs you can find. It is worth buying a whole rope of good garlic. Hang it in a cool, dry place and it will keep for months.

Marjoram: good in tomato dishes. Dries well.

Mint: fresh mint is used in *Tabbouleh* and *Tzatziki*, and as a garnish. Does not dry well.

Oregano: one of my favourite herbs. Fresh or dried, it is quite delicious in tomato dishes and sauces, and in stews.

Parsley: our British parsley is usually curly-leaved, but the Mediterranean version is flat-leaved and has a distinctively different flavour. You can buy it here in some areas; if not the curly kind will do.

Rosemary: this is a classic Italian herb for all lamb and pork dishes; use sparingly. Dries quite well.

Thyme: use on chicken and lamb before roasting or grilling, or sprinkle some of the tiny leaves into lamb casseroles. Dries well.

SPICES, with few exceptions, are best bought whole and ground as you need them. Bought ready-ground, spices quickly lose their flavour and aroma. With a pestle and mortar, you can grind the exact amount you need as and when you need it.

Allspice: adds a warm flavour to casseroles.

Capers: pickled buds which need soaking before use to remove excess saltiness.

Chillies: buy fresh or dried. Remove seeds before grinding or chopping. Dried chillies are often hotter than fresh ones – and the very small chillies are often the hottest of all!

Cinnamon: used either ground or in stick form in pilafs and Moroccan dishes.

Paprika: sweet and red, it adds depth, colour and warmth to many casseroles and stews.

Pepper: black peppercorns are best.

Saffron: expensive, so to be saved for paellas and other authentic Spanish dishes. Buy the strands if possible, and soak them in a very little water before using. Add both strands and water to the dish.

Turmeric: can give a saffron colour to a dish but the flavour is totally different and much harsher.

BREAD

The one thing I crave in Britain and can't get anywhere near where I live is bread that reminds me of the wonderful moreish breads of Spain, Italy and Greece. I suppose the nearest you can get is a stoneground wholemeal or rye bread, or a home-made loaf. Never, never, use sliced packet bread – it just won't do!

CHEESE

You can buy many Mediterranean cheeses now at larger supermarkets. For the recipes in this book, you will need Feta from Greece, Ricotta and Mozzarella from Italy – and of course, Parmesan. Parmesan is a high-fat cheese, but a little goes a long way when it is grated. Always buy Parmesan in a piece and grate it yourself; the flavour is infinitely superior to ready-grated cheese. Wrap the piece in foil and it will keep for a long time in the refrigerator.

If you want a cheese for eating with bread or salad, buy a medium-fat cheese such as Brie.

FISH

Many of the most well-known Mediterranean fishes are now widely available in Britain, but if your local fishmonger doesn't appear to stock anything other than cod and haddock, ask him if he can order other

fishes for you. Shop around and buy when prices are low; you can always freeze any surplus. Amongst my favourite white fishes, though on the expensive side, are swordfish and monkfish and my favourites for baking and grilling are mackerel, sardines and red mullet.

You can't buy a decent fish stock in a cube and it is so easy to make your own as the base of Mediterranean fish stews and soups. Just ask the fishmonger for the heads, tails and bones of fish and simmer them in water with chopped celery, carrot, leek, onion and some seasoning for 30 minutes – no more! Strain, reduce the liquid if necessary, then refrigerate or freeze.

FRUITS AND VEGETABLES

In recent years our supermarkets and corner greengrocers have recognized our craving for new varieties of fruit and vegetable, and so now virtually everything that the Mediterraneans enjoy, you can find here.

When buying, always choose the freshest produce you can. Buy from a shop that keeps its fruit and vegetables away from heat and sunlight. Refuse anything that is bruised, blackened, damaged or wrinkled. Fruits and vegetables quickly lose their vitamin C when badly stored or handled, or if kept too long. Once home, store them in cool dark conditions and use them as quickly as possible – buy little and often.

UTENSILS

Although you can easily cook almost all of the recipes in this book using equipment you undoubtedly already have at home, once you get the Mediterranean 'bug' you may like to buy a few pieces to make your life easier.

If you enjoy paella and intend to eat it regularly, the first thing I would buy is a large two-handled paella pan. Even the largest of British frying pans is not really adequate for a full paella serving four or more people, so you may have the bother of cooking in two separate pans.

A pestle and mortar is useful for grinding small

amounts of spices. Electric grinders often don't work well with small quantities.

You may like a garlic crusher, though the job is done almost as well between the flat of a spatula or knife on a chopping board.

Long, slow cooking is the secret of success for many Mediterranean stews and casseroles, and for this you really need a flameproof cast-iron casserole with a really tight-fitting lid – a Le Creuset pan, or something similar, is ideal.

As so much Mediterranean cookery involves much chopping and preparation, a set of good kitchen knives – Sabatier, for example – are a must and they should be kept well sharpened. I prefer a good sharp knife to a herb mill for chopping fresh herbs, as a mill either doesn't do the job at all or crushes the herbs to a pulp.

THE RECIPES

The recipes which follow are a selection of my favourites. All recipes serve four, but quantities for most can easily be cut or expanded to suit your numbers.

Apart from the fact that the recipes should form part of a healthy diet as described in earlier chapters my criterion when selecting them was that they should either be very easy, or at least fairly easy, to prepare and cook. After all, most of us are busy people and are not professional cooks – and that includes me! We like to provide good food and we like to entertain, but we don't have too many hours to spend doing so.

The recipes had to offer variety and they had to look nice. Most importantly for foodies, they had to taste wonderful and be satisfying.

However, don't be afraid to rely on very simple meals, such as basic pastas with plain sauces or grilled or baked fish with a few herbs and a side salad. Mediterranean food can be suitably grand when you want it to be for special occasions – or as simple as you like.

My main hope is that eating a Mediterranean-style meal – whether you have eaten it alone or, as the Mediterranean people themselves prefer to do, in the company of good friends or family on a shady terrace – will leave you smiling and feeling completely content.

OPPOSITE: Mediterranean herbs, spices and aromatic flavourings

SOUPS, STARTERS AND SNACKS

If anything really distinguishes the Mediterranean style of eating, it is the myriad of small dishes used in a variety of ways – either simply as starters, dips or snacks, or assembled together to form main courses, buffets – or even feasts. Here is a selection of the best of them.

Take a summer walk through almost any Mediterranean village, especially in the evening, and it will seem as if every resident is sitting outside. Either in cafés or on their own patios, they are sipping wine, sherry or some other favourite drink and nibbling at a variety of finger foods.

From the tapas of Spain to the meze of Greece, the Mediterraneans cherish their snacking tradition, and a parade of little starter dishes often carries on for hours.

I adore this informal way of eating, and have chosen recipes for this chapter appropriately so that you can use them in a variety of different ways. Each on its own will make a wonderful starter to a main meal. Alternatively, you can serve two or three together for an interesting light lunch, or present several at a buffet.

The dips and spreads should be served with a selection of crudités. Choose the freshest vegetables you can find, clean them carefully and cut them into strips. Carrots, peppers, mushrooms, broccoli, onions, celery and radish are all ideal. Sturdy leaves such as chicory and cos lettuce hearts also scoop up dips well. Slices of toast, strips of pitta bread or little savoury crackers may also be served as accompaniments.

If time is short, starters and snacks can be as simple as bowls of plump black olives and fresh nuts, for example. One of the nicest village meals I ever had was in Sardinia where the starter was slices of toasted bread simply sprinkled with a little garlic, olive oil, salt and pepper. In Spain you may find a similar dish, topped with soft puréed tomatoes. Even simpler is to serve crusty bread with a bowl of olive oil and crushed garlic, or the *Olive Oil and Garlic Sauce* on page 101.

Some of the dishes in the following Chapter on Suppers and Lunches also make excellent buffet fare, or they can even make good starters served in half quantities or less as appropriate.

OPPOSITE: Crab and Melon Salad (page 64)

TAPENADE
—————— *France* ——————

Tapenade keeps well in the refrigerator and is traditionally served with toast.

Calories per serving: 152
Saturated fat: Low
Protein: Low
CH: Low
Fibre: 3 g
Cholesterol: Negligible
Vitamins: C
Minerals: Iron, Calcium

225 g/8 oz stoned black olives
1 tbsp capers
1 anchovy fillet
3 tbsp olive oil
1 tsp lemon juice
$^1\!/_2$ tsp Dijon mustard
1 small clove of garlic, crushed
$^1\!/_2$ level tsp chopped bay leaf

If the olives were packed in brine, rinse them well. Soak the capers in water for 20 minutes to reduce their saltiness.

Blend all ingredients to a paste in a blender or food processor.

TZATZIKI
—————— *Greece* ——————

Perfect as a light starter with crudités, tzatziki is also often served as a side dish, especially with spicy lamb dishes.

Calories per serving: 68
Saturated fat: Low
Protein: High
Carbohydrate: Low
Fibre: Trace
Cholesterol: 3.5 mg
Vitamins: Niacin
Minerals: Calcium

1 garlic clove, crushed
10 cm/4 in piece of cucumber, finely chopped
550 ml/18 fl oz *Greek-style Yogurt* (see page 124)
handful of mint leaves, chopped
salt and black pepper

Mix the garlic and cucumber into the yogurt, season lightly and chill.

Serve sprinkled with the mint.

AUBERGINE PURÉE
—————— *Greece* ——————

Yogurt is sometimes added to this dish but I prefer the richer taste of my variation.

Calories per serving: 85
Saturated fat: Low
Protein: Low
CH: Low
Fibre: 5 g
Cholesterol: Nil
Vitamins: C, Folic acid
Minerals: Iron

2 large aubergines
2 tbsp olive oil
2 large garlic cloves, crushed
2–3 tbsp lemon juice
salt and black pepper
pinch of paprika (optional), to garnish

Bake the aubergines in an oven preheated to 190°C/375°F/gas 5, for about 45 minutes, until their skins are charred and the insides are soft.

Discard the skins and place the flesh in a blender or food processor with the oil, garlic, 2 tablespoons of the lemon juice and a little salt and pepper. Purée to a smooth paste, then taste and add more lemon juice and salt if necessary. Garnish with a little paprika, if using.

CARROT AND POTATO PURÉE
—————— *Italy* ——————

Delicious with crusty bread, this purée may also be served as a side dish to accompany a main course. It is important to use waxy, not floury, potatoes.

Calories per serving: 140
Saturated fat: Low
Protein: Low
Carbohydrate: High
Fibre: 3.5 g
Cholesterol: Nil
Vitamins: Beta-carotene, C
Minerals: Potassium, Iron

325 g/12 oz potatoes (see left), peeled and sliced
325 g/12 oz carrots, peeled and sliced
2 garlic cloves, peeled
2 tbsp olive oil
1 tbsp lemon juice
4 tsp ground cumin
pinch of cayenne
salt and black pepper

Boil the potatoes and carrots in lightly salted water with the garlic cloves until they are tender.

Drain and mash with the oil. Stir in the lemon juice, cumin and cayenne and season to taste. Serve warm or cold.

HUMMUS
—————— *Greece* ——————

Canned chickpeas give a lighter hummus, which I prefer, but you can use the dried variety.

Calories per serving: 164
Saturated fat: Low
Protein: Medium
CH: Low
Fibre: 2 g
Cholesterol: Nil
Vitamins: A, C, E, Niacin
Minerals: Iron, Potassium, Calcium

110 g/4 oz canned chickpeas *or* 50 g/2 oz dried chickpeas
3 tbsp light tahini
2 garlic cloves, crushed
juice of 2 lemons
salt
paprika, to garnish

If using canned chickpeas, rinse and drain them. If using dried chickpeas, soak them overnight. Drain and boil in fresh water for 10 minutes, then simmer for 1 or 2 hours until tender. Drain.

Purée all the ingredients in a blender or food processor. Serve at room temperature with paprika sprinkled over the top.

BEAN DIP
—————— *Italy* ——————

Fresh tender young broad beans are needed for this dish.

Calories per serving: 130
Saturated fat: Low
Protein: Low
Carbohydrate: Low
Fibre: 2.5 g
Cholesterol: 2 mg
Vitamins: Beta-carotene, C
Minerals: Iron, Calcium

225 g/8 oz shelled broad beans
2 garlic cloves, crushed
2 tbsp grated Parmesan cheese
3 tbsp olive oil

Boil the beans in lightly salted water until tender. Drain well.

Mix all ingredients to a purée in a blender or food processor, reserving a few beans.

Garnish with the reserved beans and drizzle over a little more oil.

ROAST YELLOW PEPPER DIP
——— Spain ———

This unusual dip can be spread on toast and warmed under the grill to make a quick snack.

Calories per serving: 198
Saturated fat: Medium
Protein: High
Carbohydrate: Low
Fibre: 0.5 g
Cholesterol: 24 mg
Vitamins: Beta-carotene, C
Minerals: Calcium

2 yellow peppers
100 g/3^1/$_2$ oz Feta or goats' cheese
150 g/5^1/$_2$ oz low-fat soft cheese
2 tbsp olive oil
salt and black pepper

Cook the peppers under a medium grill until they are blackened all over. Remove the skins under running water and then pat the peppers dry.

Deseed and chop the peppers coarsely. Purée them with the cheeses in a blender or food processor, then add the oil little by little with the machine still running. Season to taste.

The dip will keep for several days in the refrigerator.

LENTIL SOUP
——— France ———

There are a thousand ways to make lentil soup, but this is my particular favourite.

Calories per serving: 310
Saturated fat: Low
Protein: High
Carbohydrate: High
Fibre: 11.5 g
Cholesterol: Nil
Vitamins: C, Beta-carotene
Minerals: Iron

1^1/$_2$ tbsp olive oil
1 onion, chopped
1 leek, trimmed and chopped
325 g/12 oz green lentils
1 l/1^3/$_4$ pt vegetable stock
1 celery stalk, chopped
1 carrot, chopped
2 garlic cloves, crushed
1 bay leaf
1 tbsp chopped parsley
salt and black pepper

Heat the oil in a heavy-based saucepan over a moderate heat and sauté the onion and leek until soft.

Add the lentils and stir. Pour in the stock and bring to the boil. Lower the heat and add the remaining ingredients. Simmer for about an hour, until the lentils are soft. Adjust the seasoning.

The texture of this soup may be varied by puréeing some of it in a blender or food processor then returning this purée to the pan. The result is a thick soup which still has 'bite'

PREVIOUS PAGES: Bean Dip (page 59); Roast Yellow Pepper Dip
Hummus (page 59) Tapenade (page 58)
RIGHT: Lentil Soup

MINESTRONE SOUP
Italy

Home-made minestrone is a healthy feast which is not to be missed. Well-flavoured stock is essential.

Calories per serving: 190
Saturated fat: Low
Protein: High
Carbohydrate: Low
Fibre: 6 g
Cholesterol: 9 mg
Vitamins: C, Beta-carotene, Niacin
Minerals: Calcium, Potassium, Iron

1 large onion
2 leeks
3 celery stalks
2 carrots
175 g/6 oz white cabbage
1 tbsp olive oil
50 g/2 oz back bacon, all rind and fat removed, finely chopped
200 g/7 oz canned tomatoes
2 garlic cloves, crushed
1 l/1¾ pt chicken or ham stock
1 tsp chopped basil
50 g/ 2 oz pasta shapes
1 tsp tomato paste
2 tbsp chopped parsley
salt and black pepper
4 tbsp grated Parmesan cheese, to garnish

Finely chop all the vegetables.

Heat the oil in a large saucepan over a moderate heat and sauté the bacon for 2 minutes. Add the onion and sauté until soft. Add the celery, carrot, tomatoes, garlic and season, cover and simmer gently for 20 minutes, stirring occasionally.

Pour in the stock and basil and simmer for an hour. Add the leeks, pasta and cabbage and simmer for 30 minutes. Stir in the tomato paste and simmer for a further 10 minutes. Stir in the parsley and garnish with the Parmesan.

Variations: courgettes may be used instead of the cabbage. Pre-cooked haricot beans may also be used instead of the pasta, in which case the fibre content goes up to 9 g per serving.

RED PEPPER SOUP
Spain

Served well chilled, this dish makes a change from gazpacho.

Calories per serving: 38
Saturated fat: Low
Protein: Medium
Carbohydrate: High
Fibre: 2 g
Cholesterol: Nil
Vitamins: Beta-carotene, C
Minerals: Potassium, Iron

2 very large or 4 small red peppers
425 g/15 oz canned tomatoes
1 small garlic clove, crushed
a little tomato juice
salt and black pepper
1 tbsp chopped parsley, to garnish

Cook the peppers under a medium grill until they are blackened all over. Remove the skins under running water and pat dry.

Deseed and chop the flesh, then purée it in a blender or food processor along with the tomatoes, garlic and season to taste. If the soup is a little thick, add a little tomato juice to taste.

Serve garnished with the parsley. Chopped raw red or green peppers can also be used for garnish.

CRAB AND MELON SALAD
Italy

Calories per serving: 96
Saturated fat: Low
Protein: High
Carbohydrate: Low
Fibre: 1.25 g
Cholesterol: 50 mg
Vitamins: Beta-carotene, C
Minerals: Potassium, Calcium, Iron

4 frisée leaves
1 Ogen or Cantaloupe melon
1 large dressed crab
1 tbsp olive oil
1 tbsp lemon juice
black pepper

Arrange the frisée leaves on four serving plates. Peel and deseed the melon. Slice it into half moon shapes and divide these between the plates.

Divide the dark and light crab meat between the plates, then drizzle over the oil and lemon juice and sprinkle over plenty of black pepper.

MUSHROOMS IN GARLIC SAUCE
———— France ————

If you can't find brown cap mushrooms, ordinary white ones will do.

Calories per serving: 67
Saturated fat: Low
Protein: Low
Carbohydrate: Trace
Fibre: 1.5 g
Cholesterol: Nil
Vitamins: Niacin
Minerals: Potassium

225 g/8 oz brown cap mushrooms
2 tbsp olive oil
3 garlic cloves, finely chopped
juice of ¹/₂ lemon
salt and black pepper
2 tbsp chopped parsley, to serve

Clean the mushrooms but don't get the gills wet. Leave the caps whole and chop the stalks finely.

Heat the oil in a pan over a high heat, add the whole mushrooms along with the stalks and the garlic. Sauté for 2 or 3 minutes.

Add lemon juice and season to taste. Serve hot or cold sprinkled with the parsley.

RICOTTA-STUFFED TOMATOES
———— Italy ————

Cottage or low-fat soft cheese works equally well in this recipe.

Calories per serving: 187
Saturated fat: Medium
Protein: High
Carbohydrate: Low
Fibre: 4 g
Cholesterol: 19 mg
Vitamins: Beta-carotene, C
Minerals: Calcium, Potassium

4 beef tomatoes
200 g/7 oz Ricotta cheese
50 g/2 oz chopped walnuts
2 tbsp chopped parsley
2 mushrooms, finely chopped
2 tbsp wholemeal breadcrumbs
black pepper
4 black olives, to garnish

Preheat the oven to 180°/350°F/gas 4.

Cut the top quarter off each of the tomatoes. Scoop out the flesh and chop this and the tops and place in a bowl. Add the cheese, nuts, parsley, mushrooms, breadcrumbs and pepper. Beat together well.

Pile the mixture into the tomato shells. Place in a shallow ovenproof dish and bake for 30 minutes. Garnish with the olives to serve.

TUSCAN BEAN CASSEROLE
———— Italy ————

You can use canned beans as a shortcut in this recipe, or use all haricot beans if you prefer.

Calories per serving: 280
Saturated fat: Low
Protein: High
Carbohydrate: High
Fibre: 21 g
Cholesterol: Nil
Vitamins: Thiamin, E
Minerals: Potassium, Iron

175 g/6 oz haricot beans
175 g/6 oz kidney beans
1¹/₂ tbsp olive oil
1 large garlic clove, chopped
200 g/7 oz canned chopped
    tomatoes
1 tsp chopped fresh sage
salt and black pepper
1 tbsp chopped parsley, to garnish

Soak the beans overnight. Drain them and put them in a pan and cover them with water. Bring to the boil and boil for 10 minutes, then lower the heat and simmer for 1 hour or more until tender. Drain.

Heat the oil in a frying pan over a high heat and sauté the garlic for a few seconds. Add the cooked beans, tomatoes and sage with salt and pepper to taste. Cover and simmer for a few minutes, adding water or tomato juice if the mixture looks too dry.

Serve hot or cold, sprinkled with the chopped parsley.

BROAD BEANS AND MUSHROOMS
———— *Italy* ————

Ceps are good in this dish, but use whatever mushrooms you can find.

Calories per serving: 92
Saturated fat: Low
Protein: Medium
Carbohydrate: Low
Fibre: 4.5 g
Cholesterol: Negligible
Vitamins: C, Beta-carotene, Niacin
Minerals: Potassium, Iron

275 g/10 oz shelled broad beans
1½ tbsp olive oil
275 g/10 oz ceps, brown caps or other mushrooms, sliced if large.
1 garlic clove
1 level dsp oregano
little lemon juice
salt and black pepper
2 tbsp *Greek-style Yogurt* (see page 124)

Boil the broad beans in lightly salted water until just tender.

Heat the oil in a frying pan over a moderate heat and stir-fry the mushrooms and garlic for 2 minutes. Add the well-drained beans along with the oregano and lemon juice. Season to taste and fry for 2 more minutes, stirring all the time.

Pile the mixture into a serving dish and pour over the yogurt.

ASPARAGUS WITH LEMON SAUCE
———— *Italy* ————

Asparagus is rich in many vitamins and minerals. Choose plump spears rather than long thin ones.

Calories per serving: 150
Saturated fat: Medium
Protein: High
Carbohydrate: Low
Fibre: 2.5 g
Cholesterol: 4.5 mg
Vitamins: Beta-carotene, C, E, Folic acid
Minerals: Potassium, Iron, Calcium

24 asparagus spears (see left)
3 tbsp olive oil
juice of 1 lemon
pinch of grated nutmeg
4 tbsp grated Parmesan cheese
salt and black pepper

Tie the asparagus into four bundles with string. Place them, tips uppermost, in a tall pan containing 5 cm/2 in of water. Steam the asparagus for 10 minutes or until the tips are tender.

Meanwhile, blend the oil, lemon juice and nutmeg together well with salt and pepper to taste. Pour this mixture over the asparagus tips and then sprinkle the cheese over the top.

OPPOSITE: Asparagus with Lemon Sauce; Broad Beans and Mushrooms

LUNCHES AND SUPPERS

Mediterranean eating is, above all, a relaxed way of eating. So if you are searching for an informal supper just for one,

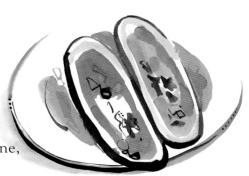

a quick meal for the family or an easy-to-prepare lunch for friends, you'll find plenty of ideal suggestions for all these in this chapter.

The essence of a supper or a lunch is informality. Whatever you choose to cook, the result should be something that can be eaten from one plate, perhaps on your knee using just a fork, and with no need for any accompaniment – apart from a glass of wine or a salad garnish.

Supper dishes should also be either quick or easy to prepare. Hence most of the recipes in this chapter will appeal to the cook in a hurry as well as to the inexperienced chef. Many of the dishes are also inexpensive, and most are suitable for vegetarians.

If you are eating alone, several recipes can be scaled down to serve one – particularly the *Pitta Pockets*, the *Melted Mozzarella and Tomato*, the *Tunisian Eggs* and the *Yogurt Kebab*.

The easiest of all Mediterranean suppers is a plate of fresh sardines, either pan-fried in a little olive oil, or brushed with oil and grilled or barbecued and served sprinkled with lemon juice and black pepper. Another very simple and quick dish is some Feta cheese crumbled over a sliced ripe beef tomato, topped with chopped parsley and eaten with a warmed pitta bread.

I have included some dishes that take slightly longer to prepare, simply because of their 'deliciousness' factor… 'The Priest Fainted' is one dish which tastes far too good to be healthy … but it is! *Pissaladina* also takes a while to cook properly, but the result is far more mouth-watering than you could possibly believe from simply glancing at its list of ingredients.

So often in the Mediterranean it *is* the simplest dish which proves to be the best. I will never forget the first time I ate a plate of melted mozzarella with tomato at a friend's house in Italy. Even if I can't quite recreate at home the atmosphere of the bougainvillaea-covered terrace on which we lunched that day, the dish never fails to delight me and fill me full of the Mediterranean spirit – even on the greyest of days here in England.

OPPOSITE: Tunisian Eggs (page 72)

PISSALADINA
——— France ———

This deceptively simple dish is quite delicious and very easy to make.

Calories per serving: 382
Saturated fat: Low
Protein: Low
Carbohydrate: Low
Fibre: 10 g
Cholesterol: 4 mg
Vitamins: C, Folic acid, Niacin
Minerals: Iron, Potassium

4 tbsp olive oil
4 thick slices of wholemeal bread, each weighing about 75 g/3 oz
900 g/2 lb onions, sliced
4 anchovy fillets
16 stoned black olives

Heat 2 tablespoons of the oil in a large pan and fry the slices of bread on one side only. Remove from the pan.

Add the remaining oil to the pan, lower the heat as far as you can and very, very slowly cook the onions until extremely soft – almost puréed. This will take up to an hour.

Preheat the oven to 190°C/375°F/gas 5.

Spread the onion purée on the untoasted side of the bread. Put them on a baking tray and bake in the oven for 10 minutes. Garnish with anchovies and olives to serve.

MELTED MOZZARELLA AND TOMATO
——— Italy ———

This is my favourite quick lunch dish, served with crusty bread to mop up the juices.

Calories per serving: 186
Saturated fat: High
Protein: High
Carbohydrate: Low
Fibre: 1.5 g
Cholesterol: 32 mg
Vitamins: Beta-carotene, C
Minerals: Calcium, Potassium

2 large beef tomatoes, sliced
225 g/8 oz Mozzarella cheese, thinly sliced
1 tbsp olive oil
1 heaped tsp dried basil *or* 12 fresh basil leaves, chopped
salt and pepper

In a shallow oval or oblong flameproof serving dish, arrange alternating slices of tomato and cheese in rows, so that half the cheese and half the tomato from each row is showing. Dribble over the oil, sprinkle on the basil and season to taste.

Flash the dish under a preheated hot grill, or cook for 30 seconds on HIGH in a microwave, until the cheese is just melting. Don't overcook the dish or the cheese will become tough.

OPPOSITE: Pissaladina

'THE PRIEST FAINTED'
—— Turkey ——

The priest apparently passed out with pure pleasure when he tasted this dish – it is that good!

Calories per serving: 196
Saturated fat: Low
Protein: Low
Carbohydrate: Medium
Fibre: 9 g
Cholesterol: Nil
Vitamins: C, Folic acid,
  Beta-carotene
Minerals: Iron

2 large aubergines
3 tbsp olive oil
1 onion, finely chopped
1 large green pepper, deseeded
425 g/15 oz canned tomatoes
1 garlic clove, chopped
50 g/2 oz raisins
1 level tsp brown sugar
pinch of ground cinnamon
100 ml/3½ fl oz tomato juice
salt and black pepper
3 tbsp chopped parsley, to garnish

Halve the aubergines and scoop out some of the flesh. Chop this and reserve it. Sprinkle some salt on the inside of the aubergine halves, turn them upside down on a plate and leave them to drain for about 30 minutes. This removes any bitterness. Rinse and pat dry.

Preheat the oven to 200°C/400°F/gas 6. Heat 2 tablespoons of the oil in a large pan over a moderate heat and sauté the halves, cut side down, for a few minutes. Transfer to a shallow ovenproof dish.

Add the remaining oil to the pan and sauté the onion until soft and slightly golden. Add the chopped aubergine and cook for a further few minutes, stirring. Add the green pepper and sauté briefly, then add the tomatoes, garlic, raisins, sugar, cinammon and seasoning to taste. Stir, and sauté for a few minutes. Add some tomato juice if the mixture looks too dry. Fill the aubergine halves with the mixture.

Cover the bottom of the baking dish with tomato juice, cover and bake for 45 minutes, or until the aubergine flesh is soft right through when tested with a skewer.

Serve cool but not chilled, with the parsley sprinkled over the top.

TUNISIAN EGGS
—— North Africa ——

Calories per serving: 170
Saturated fat: Medium
Protein: High
Carbohydrate: Low
Fibre: 2.5 g
Cholesterol: 250 mg
Vitamins: Beta-carotene, C, D, E
Minerals: Potassium, Iron

2 tbsp olive oil
1 onion, sliced
2 small green sweet peppers,
  deseeded and sliced
2 small red sweet peppers, deseeded
  and sliced
2 beef tomatoes, sliced
1 tsp ground cumin
4 large eggs
salt and black pepper
paprika, to garnish

Preheat the oven to 190°C/375°F/gas 5.

Heat the oil in a frying pan over a moderate heat and sauté the onion until soft. Add the sliced peppers and sauté for a few more minutes, stirring frequently. Add the tomatoes and sauté for another 2 minutes. Add the cumin, and season.

Transfer the mixture to a shallow ovenproof dish or 4 individual gratin dishes. Make 4 indentations in the mixture and break an egg into each. Cover and bake for 12 minutes, or until the eggs are just set. Garnish with the paprika to serve.

BAKED COURGETTES
—————— Italy ——————

This dish makes a filling supper, with some crusty bread and a tomato salad.

Calories per serving: 195
Saturated fat: High
Protein: High
Carbohydrate: Low
Fibre: 2 g
Cholesterol: 135 mg
Vitamins: Beta-carotene, C, D, E
Minerals: Iron, Calcium

675 g/1½ lb courgettes
1½ tbsp sunflower oil
1 heaped tbsp flour
2 eggs, beaten
4 tbsp skimmed milk
50 g/2 oz grated Parmesan cheese
1 tsp marjoram
2 tbsp breadcrumbs
salt and black pepper

Slice the courgettes, sprinkle them with salt and leave them to drain for about 30 minutes. Rinse and pat dry.

Preheat the oven to 190°C/375°F/gas 5.

Heat the oil in a frying pan over a moderate heat. Dust the courgettes lightly with flour and fry them in the oil until tender and golden on the outside. Transfer to paper towels, then arrange a layer of one-third of the courgette slices in the bottom of a round ovenproof dish.

Sprinkle with one-third of the marjoram. Beat together the eggs, milk, half the cheese and some salt and pepper to taste. Pour one-third of this over the courgettes. Cover with another layer of courgettes and marjoram, followed by another third of egg mixture. Repeat these layers once more. Top with the rest of the cheese and breadcrumbs and bake for 30 minutes or until the egg is set throughout and the top is golden.

STUFFED AUBERGINES
—————— Greece ——————

This makes a filling hot supper, or you could serve it cold for lunch.

Calories per serving: 345
Saturated fat: Medium
Protein: High
Carbohydrate: Low
Fibre: 8.5 g
Cholesterol: 32 mg
Vitamins: B group, C,
  Beta-carotene, E
Minerals: Iron

2 large aubergines
2 tbsp olive oil
1 large onion, finely chopped
325 g/12 oz very lean minced beef
  or lamb
425 g/15 oz canned tomatoes
225 g/8 oz (cooked weight) boiled
  brown rice
2 tsp ground cumin
2 tsp ground coriander
a little meat stock
a little tomato juice
salt and black pepper
2 tbsp chopped parsley, to garnish
2 tbsp grated Parmesan cheese, to
  garnish

Halve the aubergines and scoop out half of the flesh from each piece and chop it. Sprinkle the insides with salt and leave them to drain upside down for 30 minutes. Rinse and pat dry.

Preheat the oven to 200°C/400°G/gas 6.

Heat half the oil in a frying pan over a moderate heat and sauté the aubergine shells for 2 minutes. Remove from the pan. Add the rest of the oil to the pan and sauté the onion until soft. Add the meat and brown thoroughly. Add the aubergine flesh, the tomatoes, rice, cumin and coriander, a little meat stock, season well and simmer for a few minutes.

Stuff the aubergine shells with the mixture. Place them in a shallow ovenproof dish with a little tomato juice in the bottom, cover and bake for 1 hour, or until the aubergines are tender. Serve garnished with the parsley and Parmesan.

STUFFED PEPPERS
———— Spain ————

This dish also makes a good starter, in which case the quantity here would serve eight people.

Calories per serving: 210
Saturated fat: Low
Protein: Low
Carbohydrate: Low
Fibre: 7.5 g
Cholesterol: Nil
Vitamins: Beta-carotene, C
Minerals: Iron

1 tbsp olive oil
1 onion, finely chopped
1 garlic clove, crushed
75 g/3 oz mushrooms, chopped
1 beef tomato, chopped
50 g/2 oz (cooked weight) lentils *or* red kidney beans
1 tsp tomato paste
1 tsp dried basil
pinch of chilli powder
50 g/2 oz wholemeal breadcrumbs
a little tomato juice
4 green peppers, halved lengthwise and deseeded
salt and black pepper

Preheat the oven to 200°C/400°F/gas 6.

Heat the oil in a frying pan over a moderate heat and sauté the onion until soft and just turning golden. Add the garlic, mushrooms, chopped tomato, lentils or beans, tomato paste, basil and chilli powder. Cook for a further 10 minutes, adding extra tomato juice as necessary to keep it moist. Season, add the breadcrumbs and stir for 1 minute.

Pile the mixture into the halved peppers and place them in a shallow ovenproof dish with a little tomato juice covering the bottom. Cover and bake for 1 hour, or until the peppers are tender. Serve hot or cold.

YOGURT KEBAB
———— Turkey ————

This is one of my ten favourite Mediterranean dishes and it is so easy to make.

Calories per serving: 475
Saturated fat: Medium
Protein: High
Carbohydrate: Low
Fibre: 3 g
Cholesterol: 135 mg
Vitamins: Niacin, E, Beta-carotene, C
Minerals: Iron, Potassium, Calcium

675 g/1¹/₂ lb fillet of lamb
15 g/¹/₂ oz butter
25 g/1 oz pine nuts
1 tbsp olive oil
1 large beef tomato, skinned and chopped
1 large garlic clove, chopped
275 ml/9 fl oz *Greek-style Yogurt* (see page 124)
2 wholemeal pitta breads, halved
salt and black pepper

Cut the lamb into thin bite-sized strips.

Heat the butter in a frying pan over a moderate heat and sauté the pine nuts in it until golden. Remove from the pan and set aside. Add the olive oil to the pan and increase the heat. When it is really hot, add the lamb a few pieces at a time and brown them quickly.

Keep the browned lamb warm. Stir-fry the tomato and garlic in the remaining olive oil for 2 minutes and then transfer to a shallow serving dish. Season with salt and pepper and place the meat on top. Add any meat juices to the yogurt and warm this for a few seconds in the microwave, or in a small pan, and pour over the lamb. Scatter the pine nuts over the dish. Keep warm while toasting the halved pittas. Serve the pittas to accompany the warm lamb mixture.

You can also serve the yogurt kebab as a filling inside pitta breads, in which case the quantity of yogurt kebab here will serve 6 inside 6 whole pittas.

OPPOSITE: Yogurt Kebab

MUSSELS WITH TOMATO AND BASIL SAUCE
———— France ————

Mussels are simple to prepare and cook, and are very low in fat.

Calories per serving: 143
Saturated fat: Low
Protein: High
Carbohydrate: Low
Fibre: 1.25 g
Cholesterol: 62 mg
Vitamins: C
Minerals: Iron, Potassium, Calcium

900 g/2 lb fresh mussels in their shells
1 quantity *Tomato Sauce* (see page 101)
1 tbsp chopped fresh basil

Scrub the mussels under cold running water and pull off their beards. Discard any which are open and don't close when sharply tapped.

Make the tomato sauce, adding the extra chopped basil at the end of the cooking time.

Steam the mussels in a covered pan in a very little boiling water over a high heat. In a minute or two the shells will begin to open. Transfer the opened mussels to a serving dish, discarding any which fail to open, pour the sauce over and serve.

FETA PITTA POCKETS
———— Greece ————

Warmed filled pittas are the Mediterranean version of sandwiches.

Calories per serving: 300
Saturated fat: Medium
Protein: Medium
Carbohydrate: High
Fibre: 6 g
Cholesterol: 25 mg
Vitamins: C, A
Minerals: Iron, Calcium

4 wholemeal pitta breads
110 g/4 oz Greek Feta cheese
1 beef tomato, chopped
1 celery stalk, chopped
5 cm/2 in piece of cucumber, chopped
50 g/2 oz green pepper, chopped
6 crisp lettuce leaves, shredded
1 tbsp olive oil
a little lemon juice
$^1/_2$ tsp chopped basil
black pepper

Warm the pittas in the oven. Meanwhile, crumble the cheese and combine it with the rest of the ingredients.

Fill the pittas with the mixture and serve.

TUNA PITTA POCKETS
———— Greece ————

Calories per serving: 276
Saturated fat: Low
Protein: High
Carbohydrate: High
Fibre: 6.5 g
Cholesterol: 20 mg
Vitamins: Niacin, E, C
Minerals: Iron, Calcium

4 wholemeal pitta breads
200 g/7 oz canned tuna in oil, drained and flaked
1 beef tomato, chopped
1 small onion, finely chopped
110 g/4 oz canned cannellini beans, drained
1 tbsp chopped parsley
1 tbsp olive oil
1 tbsp white wine vinegar
black pepper

Warm the pittas in the oven. Meanwhile, combine the rest of the ingredients.

Fill the pittas with the tuna mixture and serve.

OPPOSITE: Mussels with Tomato and Basil Sauce

MAIN COURSES

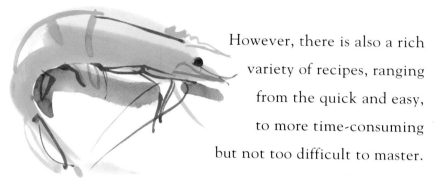

Mediterranean meals often
consist of simple grilled,
baked or roast fish,
poultry or meat, served with
salads and bread or potatoes.

However, there is also a rich
variety of recipes, ranging
from the quick and easy,
to more time-consuming
but not too difficult to master.

By no means all Mediterranean main course dishes are quick to prepare and cook. One of the dishes that, for me, most sums up traditional Mediterranean cooking is the delicious Greek *stiphado* of beef or rabbit which takes several hours of long, slow cooking in the oven to be at its most meltingly tender and succulent.

However, one of the reasons that I – an amateur cook and busy working mother – don't mind planning ahead to enjoy dishes such as this or, for instance, the *Moroccan Couscous*, is that the meals are unpretentious, the techniques are simple...and there is very little to go wrong. Although there is often much chopping and amalgamating involved, there is nothing to *worry* about in the Mediterranean kitchen.

The recipes in this chapter reflect the relaxed attitude of the average Mediterranean cook – usually the housewife. There are dozens of different variations on these recipes, depending upon whose

kitchen you are in at the time, so don't be afraid to experiment a little when you can.

Of course, many Mediterranean main courses need no recipe at all. What could be a better meal than a fresh whole red mullet or a swordfish steak baked in a foil parcel with some chopped fresh herbs, lemon juice and black pepper?

Traditionally, meat was a rare commodity in the Mediterranean area. When available, it was 'stretched', as in the recipes in the following chapter. But pork chops, lamb kebabs and roasts cooked over an open fire are all part of the tradition of special occasions and should be enjoyed to the full every now and then without any feelings of guilt!

As most of the main course dishes are high in protein, they need a high-carbohydrate accompaniment, such as potatoes, rice or pasta, and salad or vegetables. If you are following one of the Plans in chapters 3 or 4, you will find suitable suggestions for accompaniments there.

OPPOSITE: Honeyed Chicken (page 86)

SULTANA-BAKED SARDINES
—— Italy ——

Serve the sardines with a green salad and a few plain boiled potatoes.

Pine nuts make an excellent alternative to the almonds.

Calories per serving: 460
Saturated fat: Low
Protein: High
Carbohydrate: Low
Fibre: 1.5 g
Cholesterol: 170 mg
Vitamins: E, the B complex
Minerals: Iron, Calcium

12 good-sized fresh sardines
25 g/1 oz blanched almonds
2 tbsp wholemeal breadcrumbs
2 tbsp sultanas
1 lemon
12 small bay leaves
1 tbsp olive oil
salt and black pepper

Preheat the oven to 180°C/350°F/gas 4.

Top, tail and split open the sardines. Remove their backbones and flatten the fish carefully.

Chop the nuts and mix them with the breadcrumbs, sultanas and the juice of half the lemon. Season to taste and spoon the mixture over 6 of the sardines. Place 2 bay leaves on each and top with the remaining sardines. Cut each in two.

Pack the sardines closely in a shallow ovenproof dish. Sprinkle over the oil and bake for about 30 minutes. Serve with the remaining lemon, cut in slices.

SWORDFISH STEAKS WITH ALMOND SAUCE
—— Spain ——

The Spanish love almonds, and this rich yet delicate sauce is one of the wonders of their cuisine. Serve the sauce cold to accompany grilled steaks.

Calories per serving: 438
Saturated fat: Low
Protein: High
Carbohydrate: Low
Fibre: 3 g
Cholesterol: 140 mg
Vitamins: E, C, Beta-carotene
Minerals: Iron, Calcium

1 dried hot pepper
75 g/3 oz blanched almonds
225 g/8 oz canned tomatoes
1 tsp paprika
1 garlic clove, chopped
4 tbsp olive oil
2 tbsp red wine vinegar
4 swordfish steaks, each weighing
    about 175 g/6 oz
little tomato juice
salt

Deseed the pepper and soak it in a little water for a few minutes. Toast the almonds in a hot oven until golden then grind them finely in a coffee mill, taking care not to over-grind.

Blend the tomatoes with the paprika, garlic and seasoning in a food processor and gradually add all but 1 tablespoon of the olive oil. Stir in the vinegar.

Brush the swordfish steaks with the remaining olive oil and cook them under a preheated moderate grill.

Stir the almonds into the tomato sauce. If the sauce seems too thick, add a little tomato juice to taste and stir again.

KING PRAWN SKEWERS
—— Italy ——

Calories per serving: 180
Saturated fat: Low
Protein: High
Carbohydrate: Low
Fibre: Nil
Cholesterol: 215 mg
Vitamins: Niacin, Folic acid
Minerals: Calcium, Potassium

24 uncooked giant king prawns in
    their shells
2 tbsp olive oil
2 tbsp lemon juice
salt and black pepper
lemon wedges, to serve

Remove the heads from the prawns but leave their tails. Divide them between 4 small skewers and place these in a shallow dish. Sprinkle with the oil and lemon juice and a little salt and pepper. Leave to marinate for 1 hour, turning a few times.

Grill the skewers for a few minutes, basting with the juices from the dish. Serve with lemon wedges.

SPICY MONKFISH KEBABS
—————— Greece ——————

Monkfish is the perfect fish for kebabs as its firm meaty flesh does not break up.

Calories per serving: 345
Saturated fat: Medium
Protein: High
Carbohydrate: Low
Fibre: 3 g
Cholesterol: 120 mg
Vitamins: C, Beta-carotene, Niacin
Minerals: Potassium

675 g/1¹/₂ lb monkfish fillet, cubed
24 button mushrooms
1 large, or 2 small, green peppers
4 slices of lean rindless bacon
8 bay leaves
for the sauce:
425 g/15 oz canned tomatoes
1 heaped tbsp tomato paste
1 large garlic clove, crushed
2 tbsp olive oil
1 generous tbsp runny honey
2 tbsp red wine vinegar
1 tsp chilli sauce
1 tbsp soya sauce
1 heaped tsp oregano

Heat the sauce ingredients together in a pan, stirring thoroughly. Simmer gently while preparing the kebabs.

Deseed the peppers and cut them and the bacon into squares.

Using 4 long kebab skewers or 8 short ones, arrange the fish, mushrooms, pieces of pepper and bacon and the bay leaves alternately on the skewers. Brush with a little sauce and grill under a moderate heat for about 10 minutes, turning at least once and basting again, until the fish is golden and the peppers slightly charred.

Add the juices from the grill pan to the sauce and stir before serving.

SCALLOPS WITH MUSHROOMS
—————— France ——————

Calories per serving: 220
Saturated fat: Low
Protein: High
Carbohydrate: Low
Fibre: 1.5 g
Cholesterol: 48 mg
Vitamins: C
Minerals: Iron, Potassium

2 tbsp olive oil
550 g/20 oz prepared scallops, cut across in half horizontally
3 garlic cloves, crushed
24 button mushrooms, halved
4 tbsp full-bodied dry white wine
4 tbsp chopped parsley
salt and black pepper

Heat the oil in a frying pan over a moderate heat, add the scallops and sauté them for 2–3 minutes only – scallops hate to be overcooked!

Add the garlic and mushrooms, stir for 30 seconds only, add the wine, parsley and seasoning, bubble gently for a few seconds and serve.

SQUID IN RED WINE
—————— Spain ——————

Squid is easily available ready-prepared.

Calories per serving: 370
Saturated fat: Low
Protein: High
Carbohydrate: Low
Fibre: 1.5 g
Cholesterol: 120 mg
Vitamins: Niacin, B12, A, C
Minerals: Iron, Potassium

2 tbsp olive oil
1 large onion, thinly sliced
2 garlic cloves, chopped
squid, weighing about 1 k/2¹/₄ lb, cleaned and cut into strips
2 beef tomatoes, skinned and chopped
1 tsp oregano
1 bay leaf
1 dsp tomato paste
1 glass of red wine
1 tsp cornflour
salt and black pepper

Heat the oil in a frying pan which has a lid and sauté the onion, uncovered, until transparent and just turning golden. Add the garlic and squid slices and sauté for a few minutes – no longer!

Add the tomatoes, herbs, seasonings and tomato paste, stir and cook for a minute. Add the wine and allow to bubble and simmer for 2 minutes.

Mix the cornflour with a very little cold water and add to the pan. Stir, cover and simmer very gently for 45 minutes or until the squid is tender and the sauce is rich.

OVERLEAF: King Prawn Skewers and Swordfish Steaks with Almond Sauce

PRAWNS PROVENÇAL
—— France ——

Calories per serving: 203
Saturated fat: Low
Protein: High
Carbohydrate: Low
Fibre: 1.5 g
Cholesterol: 162 mg
Vitamins: C, Beta-carotene
Minerals: Calcium, Potassium

2 tbsp olive oil
1 onion, finely chopped
2 garlic cloves, chopped
425 g/15 oz canned tomatoes
1 large glass of dry white wine
1 small chilli seeded and chopped
1 bay leaf
325 g/12 oz peeled cooked prawns
black pepper
2 tbsp chopped parsley, to garnish

Heat the oil in a frying pan over a moderate heat and sauté the onion in it until soft and just turning golden. Add the garlic and stir for a few seconds. Add the tomatoes, wine, chilli, bay leaf and pepper. Simmer for about 30 minutes, until it becomes a rich sauce.

Just before serving, add the prawns and simmer gently for a few minutes. Sprinkle the parsley over the dish to serve.

BAKED SEA BASS
—— Greece ——

If sea bass is not available, use swordfish, cod or halibut.

Calories per serving: 425
Saturated fat: Low
Protein: High
Carbohydrate: Low
Fibre: 3.5 g
Cholesterol: 150 mg
Vitamins: Beta-carotene, C
Minerals: Calcium, Potassium

2 tbsp olive oil
1 large onion, sliced
2 carrots, sliced
2 celery stalks, chopped
1 large garlic clove, crushed
2 beef tomatoes, skinned and
    chopped
1 small glass of dry white wine
4 sea bass steaks, each weighing
    about 225 g/8 oz
salt and black pepper

Preheat the over to 180°C/350°F/gas 4.

Heat the oil in a frying pan and sauté the onion until transparent. Add the carrot and celery and stir for a few minutes. Add the garlic and a small glass of water, and season. Cover and simmer for 10 minutes. Add the tomatoes and simmer for a few minutes, then add the wine. Simmer gently for a few seconds. Put the fish in an oiled baking dish, cover with sauce and bake for 30 minutes.

SARDINIAN SEAFOOD STEW
—— Sardinia ——

The fish and seafood can vary according to availability: my favourite mix is red mullet, sea bream and rock salmon with shelled scallops, peeled cooked prawns and squid cut into strips.

Calories per serving: 490
Saturated fat: Low
Protein: High
Carbohydrate: Low
Fibre: 3 g
Cholesterol: 227 mg
Vitamins: Beta-carotene, C, E
Minerals: Iron, Calcium

4 tbsp olive oil
2 onions, finely chopped
1 leek, finely chopped
4 garlic cloves
4 canned tomatoes, deseeded
1 tsp dried fennel
1 large bay leaf
1 sachet of saffron
piece of orange peel
1.1 1/2 pt fish stock
1.8 k/4 lb assorted fish (see left),
    cut into chunks
675 g/1½ lb seafood (see left)
2 tbsp chopped parsley
salt and black pepper

Heat the oil in a flameproof casserole over a moderate heat. Sauté the onions and leek in it until they are soft and just golden. Add the garlic and tomatoes and simmer for 2 minutes. Add the herbs and spices, orange peel and stock, season and bring to the boil. Beat to emulsify.

Reduce the heat and add any firm-fleshed fish, such as mullet and bream. Simmer for 5 minutes, then add the seafood and any soft-fleshed fish, such as rock salmon. Simmer for 3 more minutes.

Immediately transfer the seafood and fish to a serving dish. Pour over some of the stock and sprinkle with the parsley.

OPPOSITE: Sardinian Seafood Stew

CHICKEN WITH 30 CLOVES OF GARLIC
———— France ————

If the garlic cloves are properly cooked they become mellow and deliciously nutty.

Calories per serving: 400
Saturated fat: Medium
Protein: High
Carbohydrate: Low
Fibre: 1 g
Cholesterol: 180 mg
Vitamins: Niacin, Folic acid, C
Minerals: Iron, Potassium

1 small roasting chicken
30 large cloves of Provençal garlic, unpeeled
1 dsp garlic paste (optional)
juice of 1 lemon, plus $1/4$ lemon
4 sprigs of fresh thyme *or* 1 tsp dried thyme
15 g/$1/2$ oz butter
1 tbsp olive oil
salt and black pepper

Preheat the oven to 200°C/400°F/gas 6.

Put the chicken on a piece of foil large enough to make a loose parcel. Arrange the garlic cloves on either side. Put some of the garlic paste, if using, and a wedge of lemon inside the bird with some salt and pepper. Spread any remaining garlic paste on the breasts of the chicken and sprinkle the thyme and a little more salt and pepper over. Dab the butter on the breasts and finally pour over the olive oil and lemon juice. Make a parcel, folding the foil together along the top of the chicken.

Roast for $1^{1}/4$ hours, then loosen the foil and return to the oven for 15 minutes more to let the chicken brown.

Serve the chicken with the whole garlic cloves and the juices from inside the parcel.

HONEYED CHICKEN
———— Spain ————

For an even less calorific dish, remove the skin from the chicken breasts.

Calories per serving: 370
Saturated fat: Medium
Protein: High
Carbohydrate: Low
Fibre: Trace
Cholesterol: 100 mg
Vitamins: Niacin, C
Minerals: Iron

4 chicken breasts
2 tbsp olive oil
1 onion, finely chopped
3 tbsp runny honey
1 level tsp dried rosemary *or* 1 sprig of grated rind of 1 lemon
1 large glass of dry white wine
6 anchovy fillets, rinsed
salt and black pepper

Preheat the oven to 170°C/335°F/gas 3-4.

Season the chicken portions with salt and pepper, Heat the oil in a frying pan and sauté the chicken until the skin is golden. Transfer to an ovenproof casserole.

Sauté the onion in the pan until soft and add that to the casserole.

Combine the lemon rind, honey and rosemary in a small pan and warm through. Pour this mixture over the contents of the casserole and bake for 30 minutes.

At the end of this time, add the wine and anchovies and return to the oven for a further 15 minutes, or until the chicken is tender.

CHICKEN WITH PINE NUTS
—————— Spain ——————

Calories per serving: 425
Saturated fat: Low
Protein: High
Carbohydrate: Low
Fibre: 3 g
Cholesterol: 112 mg
Vitamins: Beta-carotene, C, E
Minerals: Iron, Potassium

2 tbsp olive oil
4 chicken breast fillets, skinned and cut into 4
1 onion, finely chopped
1 red pepper, deseeded and chopped
1 garlic clove, chopped
1 tsp flour
1 tbsp chopped parsley
25 g/1 oz pine nuts
large glass of dry Spanish sherry
salt and black pepper

Heat the oil in a frying pan over a high heat and sauté the chicken for 1 minute to brown each side. Remove and keep warm.

Sauté the onion until soft, add the pepper and sauté for a few minutes more. Add the garlic, stir and add the flour, salt and pepper. Stir and add the parsley, pine nuts, chicken and sherry.

Simmer for 10 minutes, or until the chicken is cooked through, adding a little water or chicken stock if the dish looks too dry.

SOUVLAKIA
—————— Greece ——————

Often the simplest dishes taste the best, and this is simply delicious.

Calories per serving: 390
Saturated fat: Medium
Protein: High
Carbohydrate: Low
Fibre: Trace
Cholesterol: 128 mg
Vitamins: Niacin, B12
Minerals: Iron, Potassium

675 g/1½ lb fillet of lamb, cut into small cubes
16 bay leaves
3 tbsp olive oil
2 tbsp lemon juice
2 tsp oregano
salt and black pepper
1 lemon, cut into wedges, to serve

Soak 8 small wooden skewers well in water. Thread the lamb on the skewers, with a bay leaf at either end.

Lay the skewers in a shallow dish and dribble over the oil and lemon juice. Sprinkle on the oregano and salt and pepper and leave to marinate for 1–2 hours, turning from time to time.

Cook the skewers under a hot grill, basting once or twice and serve with lemon wedges.

The skewers go well with *Tzatziki* (page 58) and a plain tomato and onion salad.

ROAST LAMB
—————— Greece ——————

In Greece the lamb is roast very slowly for hours, until it virtually falls off the bone.

Calories per serving: 460
Saturated fat: Medium
Protein: High
Carbohydrate: Low
Fibre: Nil
Cholesterol: 128 mg
Vitamins: Niacin, B12
Minerals: Iron, Potassium

4 tbsp olive oil
2 tbsp runny honey
2 dsp crushed dried rosemary
2 garlic cloves, crushed
4 thick lamb steaks on the bone, cut from the leg

Preheat the oven to 160°C/325°F/gas 3.

Mix the oil, honey, rosemary and garlic thoroughly in a small bowl and coat the lamb steaks with the mixture.

Put the steaks in a roasting pan and roast for 2 hours, basting from time to time, until lamb is a rich dark colour and falls easily from the bone.

If you have the time you can roast at a lower temperature for a longer time for even better results.

LAMB IN WHITE WINE
———— Greece ————

This tastes even better if kept overnight and reheated the next day.

Calories per serving: 375
Saturated fat: Medium
Protein: High
Carbohydrate: Low
Fibre: 0.5 g
Cholesterol: 128 mg
Vitamins: Niacin, B12,
  Beta-carotene
Minerals: Iron, Potassium

2 tbsp olive oil
675 g/1½ lb fillet of lamb, cubed
1 garlic clove, finely chopped
½ glass of dry white wine
2 tbsp lemon juice
200 g/7 oz canned tomatoes
1 tbsp chopped parsley
salt and black pepper

Heat the oil in a frying pan over a high heat and sauté the lamb a little at a time until uniformly brown.

Turn down the heat and add the garlic. Sauté briefly. Return the lamb to the pan and add the wine, lemon juice, tomatoes and parsley. Season and simmer for 10 minutes, adding a little water if necessary.

LAMB AND APRICOT CASSEROLE
———— Morocco ————

Try replacing half the apricots with chopped dates or sultanas for a different flavour.

Calories per serving: 450
Saturated fat: Medium
Protein: High
Carbohydrate: Low
Fibre: 9 g
Cholesterol: 130 mg
Vitamins: Niacin, B12, C,
  Beta-carotene
Minerals: Iron, Potassium

1 tbsp olive oil
675 g/1½ lb fillet of lamb, cubed
1 large onion, chopped
1 large green pepper, deseeded and
  sliced
1 dsp flour
110 g/4 oz canned chickpeas
1 sachet of saffron
about 500 ml/16 fl oz good meat
  stock
1 tsp allspice
110 g/4 oz dried apricots
1 tbsp lemon juice
salt and black pepper

Preheat the oven to 180°C/350°F/gas 4.

Heat the oil in a flameproof casserole over a high heat and brown the lamb a little at a time. Remove and keep warm.

Add the onions and peppers to the casserole and sauté them until soft. Return the meat to the pan. Add the flour, stir and add the chickpeas, saffron, salt, pepper and allspice along with just enough stock to cover the meat.

Cover and bake for 1 hour, then add the apricots and lemon juice. Add a little more stock if the sauce is looking too dry. Return the casserole to the oven for 15 minutes more. Adjust the seasoning, if necessary, before serving. .

OPPOSITE: Lamb and Apricot Casserole

FILLET OF PORK MARSALA
—————— Italy ——————

The traditional recipe does not contain the yogurt, but I find it makes a much nicer sauce.

Calories per serving: 275
Saturated fat: High
Protein: High
Carbohydrate: Low
Fibre: Nil
Cholesterol: 110 mg
Vitamins: B group
Minerals: Potassium, Iron

4 fillets of pork, each weighing
    about 175 g/6 oz
2 tbsp corn oil
1 glass of Marsala wine
2 tbsp *Greek-style Yogurt* (see page
    124)
salt and black pepper

Slice each tenderloin of pork into 3 or 4 medallions. Heat the oil in a frying pan over a high heat and brown the medallions for 1 minute on each side.

Add the Marsala, season with salt and pepper and bubble briefly. Reduce the heat and simmer for a few minutes, until the pork is cooked through.

Transfer the pork to serving plates. Stir the yogurt into the pan juices, adjust the seasoning and pour over the pork to serve.

PORK WITH ORANGES
—————— Spain ——————

Calories per serving: 256
Saturated fat: High
Protein: High
Carbohydrate: Low
Fibre: Trace
Cholesterol: 110 mg
Vitamins: B group, C
Minerals: Potassium, Iron

1 tbsp olive oil
4 fillets of pork, each weighing
    about 175 g/6 oz
2 glasses of dry sherry
grated rind of 2 oranges
2 tbsp orange juice
3 tbsp chicken stock
1/2 tsp ground ginger
salt and black pepper

Heat the oil in a frying pan over a high heat and brown the pork fillets for 1 minute each side.

Add the sherry and allow to bubble. Turn the heat down and add the rest of the ingredients. Season well and simmer, covered, for about 20 minutes.

RABBIT STIPHADO
—————— Greece ——————

You can use lean beef instead of the rabbit, in which case there will be 350 calories and 84 mg cholesterol per serving.

Calories per serving: 280
Saturated fat: Medium
Protein: High
Carbohydrate: Low
Fibre: 3 g
Cholesterol: 70 mg
Vitamins: B12, Niacin, C,
   Beta-carotene
Minerals: Iron, Potassium

1 large rabbit or 2 small rabbits,
    cut into pieces (or 550 g/1 1/4 lb
    lean braising steak)
675 g/1 1/2 lb small onions, peeled
    but left whole
425 g/15 oz canned tomatoes
3 garlic cloves, crushed
2 bay leaves
salt and black pepper
for the marinade:
4 small glasses of robust red wine
4 tbsp red wine vinegar
2 tbsp olive oil
a few black peppercorns
1 tsp allspice

Mix together the marinade ingredients in an ovenproof casserole and add the rabbit pieces. Cover and leave for several hours or overnight.

Preheat the oven to 160°C/325°F/gas 3.

Pour off a little of the marinade and reserve. Add the onions, tomatoes, garlic, bay leaves and seasoning to the casserole. Pour back just enough of the marinade barely to cover the meat. Cover and cook in the oven for 5 hours.

OPPOSITE: Pork with Oranges

PASTA AND GRAINS

Pasta and grains are the basis of many Mediterranean dishes. Together they supply a high percentage of the carbohydrates that make

up a large part of a healthy diet. No one need feel guilty about indulging in a plate of steaming spaghetti or a spiced rice dish.

Pasta has a totally unfair reputation outside of Italy for being 'fattening'. This is probably because in the typical *trattoria* in this country you will find pasta dishes which are brimming with cream, butter, cheese and meat.

However, this is not how pasta is traditionally eaten. Even today, in Southern Italy, you will find a big pot of boiled pasta, served for the family with only a little tomato sauce or, even simpler, with a trickle of olive oil, some black pepper and a sprinkling of grated Parmesan – a cheese which goes a very long way! With a side salad accompaniment, this is a perfect meal all year round.

The pasta sauces in this chapter vary from light to rich-tasting. However, the richness comes from the flavourful Mediterranean vegetables, nuts, and so on, that I have used rather than from any high-saturated-fat additions.

Wholewheat pasta can be used in any of the recipes, but I must confess that I prefer the hard durum wheat pasta, as beloved by the Italians themselves. It contains slightly less fibre than wholewheat pasta, but the difference really is not enough to worry about.

For the grain dishes, I have chosen (my own versions of) the classics: the paellas, risottos and pilafs of the Mediterranean are wonderful dishes which are very familiar to us all. North African *Couscous* is less well-known; the light, almost fluffy couscous grain with its accompanying stew makes a marvellous dinner party meal which is easily adapted for large numbers.

Plain boiled rice or pasta can be served instead of bread or potatoes with any meal. Rice can be enlivened by adding saffron or turmeric, chopped herbs or tiny pieces of fruit or vegetables for added colour, taste and texture. Pasta needs nothing other than cooking until it is just *al dente* and remember always to add a little oil to the cooking water to prevent it sticking together.

OPPOSITE: Couscous (page 95)

93

TOMATO AND MUSHROOM RISOTTO
—————— Italy ——————

Risottos are remarkably adaptable and this is a simple one to get you started.

Calories per serving: 440
Saturated fat: Low
Protein: Medium
Carbohydrate: High
Fibre: 5.5 g
Cholesterol: 9 mg
Vitamins: C, Beta-carotene
Minerals: Potassium, Calcium

425 g/15 oz canned tomatoes, chopped
1 tbsp tomato paste
3 tbsp olive oil
1 onion, finely chopped
1 garlic clove, chopped
325 g/12 oz brown cap mushrooms
275 g/10 oz Arborio rice
800 ml/28 fl oz vegetable stock
5 chopped fresh basil leaves *or* 2 tsp dried basil
2 tbsp chopped parsley
salt and black pepper
8 tbsp grated Parmesan cheese, to serve

Mix the tomatoes with the tomato paste in a bowl. Heat the oil in a large frying pan over a moderate heat and sauté the onion until soft and just turning golden. Add the garlic and stir for 30 seconds. Add the mushrooms and stir again. Add the rice, stir, and then pour in the tomatoes with half of the stock. Season and add the herbs.

Bring to the boil and then lower the heat and simmer gently. If the liquid all gets absorbed, add a little more. Continue simmering for up to 45 minutes, adding more liquid as necessary, until the rice is creamy, moist and tender. Serve sprinkled with the cheese.

LAMB PILAF
—————— Turkey ——————

I have used risotto rice for this recipe, but you could use long-grain or brown rice.

Calories per serving: 575
Saturated fat: Low
Protein: High
Carbohydrate: Medium
Fibre: 6 g
Cholesterol: 64 mg
Vitamins: Niacin, B12, E, C
Minerals: Iron, Potassium, Calcium

2 tbsp corn oil
1 large onion, finely chopped
325 g/12 oz fillet of lamb, cut into small pieces
275 g/10 oz Arborio rice
1 small aubergine, chopped
about 800 ml/28 fl oz chicken stock
1 beef tomato, deseeded and chopped
2 tbsp currants
2 tbsp raisins
2 tbsp pine nuts
1 tbsp blanched almonds, chopped
1 garlic clove, chopped
1 tsp allspice
salt and pepper

Heat the oil in a large frying pan over a moderate heat and sauté the onion until soft and transparent. Add the lamb and stir for a minute. Add the rice and stir well, then add the aubergine and stir again. Add the stock and the remaining ingredients and simmer until the rice is tender and creamy and has absorbed all the liquid. (Add more stock as necessary during the cooking).

COUSCOUS
— Morocco —

Virtually all couscous available in this country is pre-cooked and easy to prepare.

This serves 4 very hungry people and could easily serve 6 as part of a three-course meal, in which case it would be 460 calories per serving.

You can use a whole jointed chicken for the couscous instead of breast portions and make a chicken stock with the carcass to use instead of water in this recipe.

Calories per serving: 690
Saturated fat: Low
Protein: High
Carbohydrate: Medium
Fibre: 7 g
Cholesterol: 87 mg
Vitamins: Beta-carotene, Niacin, C, A, E
Minerals: Iron, Potassium

3 tbsp olive oil
4 chicken breasts, skinned
2 onions, quartered
2 carrots, quartered
4 small turnips, topped and tailed
1 tbsp tomato paste
1 beef tomato, chopped
110 g/4 oz canned chickpeas
1 large garlic clove, chopped
1 tsp turmeric
1 tsp ground coriander
1 tsp ground cumin
275 g/10 oz pre-cooked couscous
15 g/½ oz butter
salt and black pepper
1½ tbsp toasted almonds, to garnish
1½ tbsp raisins, to garnish
2 tbsp chopped parsley, to garnish

Heat 1 tablespoon of the oil in a large heavy stew-pan over a moderate heat and sauté the chicken for a minute until slightly golden. Add water to cover, bring to boil and skim off any froth that appears on the top. Add the onions, carrot, turnip, tomato paste, tomato, half the chickpeas, the garlic, turmeric, coriander, cumin, seasoning and any extra water needed barely to cover the vegetables. Simmer for 20 minutes.

Meanwhile soak the couscous in a bowl of water for 20 minutes, then drain and put in a saucepan with 2 tablespoons of water and the rest of the chickpeas. Heat gently, stirring frequently but gently.

When the meat and vegetables are ready, stir the butter into the couscous, along with the remaining olive oil and a few tablespoons of the vegetable broth. Pile it on a serving plate and make a well in the centre.

Using a slotted spoon, transfer the chicken from the pan and arrange it in the well in the centre of the couscous. Garnish with the almonds, raisins and parsley and serve the broth and vegetables in a separate bowl for guests to help themselves.

RICE WITH PEPPERS AND PORK
— Spain —

This is similar to a risotto, but traditional risottos never use long-grain rice or saffron.

Calories per serving: 396
Saturated fat: Low
Protein: High
Carbohydrate: High
Fibre: 3 g
Cholesterol: 55 mg
Vitamins: Niacin, B12, Beta-carotene, C
Minerals: Potassium, Iron

1 tbsp olive oil
325 g/12 oz fillet of pork, cut into small cubes
1 onion, finely chopped
3 garlic cloves, chopped
1 red and 1 yellow or green pepper, deseeded and chopped
200 g/7 oz canned tomatoes
1 tbsp chopped parsley
1 sachet of saffron
275 g/10 oz long-grain rice
600 ml/21 fl oz vegetable stock
salt and black pepper

Heat the oil in a flameproof casserole over a high heat and brown the pork a little at a time. Remove and keep warm.

Lower the heat, add the onion and sauté it until transparent. Return the meat to the pan, add the garlic and stir for 30 seconds. Add the peppers, tomatoes, parsley, seasoning and saffron and simmer for 20 minutes.

Add the rice and stock, stir and bring to boil, then lower the heat and simmer for 20 minutes, or until most of the liquid is absorbed and the rice is tender.

PAELLA
———— Spain ————

For the paella to be authentic, you really do need to use some fresh shellfish and at least some of the prawns should be left with their tails on. The whole point of paella is the lovely saffron flavour so use the best.

Calories per serving: 685
Saturated fat: Low
Protein: High
Carbohydrate: Low
Fibre: 8 g
Cholesterol: 278 mg
Vitamins: Beta-carotene, Niacin, C, E
Minerals: Calcium, Potassium, Iron

20 fresh mussels in their shells (or 140 g/5 oz shelled frozen mussels, defrosted)
4 small chicken breast fillets,
1 small tomato
1 red pepper
1 green pepper
2 sachets of saffron strands
2 tbsp olive oil
1 small onion, very finely chopped
1 tsp paprika
800 ml/28 fl oz chicken stock
275 g/10 oz long-grain rice
110 g/4 oz freshly boiled (or defrosted frozen) small peas
8 jumbo prawns with their tails
200 g/7 oz shelled cooked prawns
salt and black pepper

Scrub the mussels and remove their beards. Discard any that don't close when you tap them sharply.

Skin the chicken fillets and cut them in 4. Deseed and chop the tomato and peppers. Soak the saffron strands in a little water.

Heat the oil in a very large frying pan or paella pan over a moderate heat and sauté the chicken pieces for a minute or two until golden. Add the tomato, peppers, onion, saffron, paprika and seasoning together with a little stock and simmer for about 15 minutes.

Add the rice, peas, the large prawns and more stock. Simmer until the rice is tender, adding more stock as required.

Stir in the prawns, then add the mussels. When they open, the paella is ready.

VEGETABLE LASAGNE
———— Italy ————

The lasagne can be varied by using sliced mushrooms in place of the courgettes.

Calories per serving: 400
Saturated fat: Low
Protein: High
Carbohydrate: Low
Fibre: 8 g
Cholesterol: 133 mg
Vitamins: Beta-carotene, A, C, E
Minerals: Iron, Calcium

1 small aubergine, sliced
225 g/8 oz courgettes, sliced
110 g/4 oz (dry weight) brown lentils, washed
2 tbsp olive oil
1 onion, chopped
425 g/15 oz canned tomatoes
1 large green pepper, deseeded and chopped
1 tsp oregano
300 ml/^{1}/$_2$ pt vegetable stock
8 sheets 'no-cook' lasagne verdi
2 eggs
4 tbsp skimmed milk
300 ml/^{1}/$_2$ pint *Greek-style Yogurt* (see page 124)
4 tbsp grated Parmesan cheese
salt and black pepper

Put the aubergines and courgettes in a colander and sprinkle with salt. Leave to drain for 30 minutes, rinse and pat dry. Boil the lentils for about 1 hour, until tender.

Preheat the oven to 190°C/375°F/gas 5.

Heat the oil in a frying pan over a moderate heat and sauté the onion for a few minutes until soft. Add the courgettes and aubergines and stir-fry for a few minutes. Add the tomatoes, pepper, drained lentils, oregano, seasoning and a little stock. Cover and simmer for 20 minutes. Add more stock until the mixture is fairly liquid as 'no-cook' lasagne absorbs a lot of liquid.

In a suitable ovenproof dish, spread a layer of half the mixture followed by 4 sheets of lasagne, then the remaining vegetables and lasagne. Beat the eggs and milk in a bowl. Stir in the yogurt. Pour over the lasagne and sprinkle over the cheese. Bake for 40 minutes.

OPPOSITE: Paella

RICOTTA AND AUBERGINE SAUCE
—————— Italy ——————

This sauce combines well with pasta shells or spaghetti.

Calories per serving: 196
Saturated fat: Low
Protein: Low
Carbohydrate: Low
Fibre: 4 g
Cholesterol: 9 mg
Vitamins: Beta-carotene, C
Minerals: Iron, Calcium

1 aubergine, chopped
2 tbsp olive oil
1 quantity *Tomato Sauce* (see page 101)
100 g/3¹/₂ oz Ricotta cheese

Sprinkle the chopped aubergine with salt and leave to drain for 30 minutes in a colander. Rinse and pat dry.

Heat the oil in a frying pan over a moderate heat and sauté the aubergine, stirring, until fairly soft. Add the tomato sauce and simmer for 30 minutes.

Just before serving, add the cheese to the sauce.

MUSHROOM SAUCE
—————— Italy ——————

Mushroom sauce is a perfect accompaniment to fettucine or tagliatelle.

Calories per serving: 85
Saturated fat: Low
Protein: Low
Carbohydrate: Low
Fibre: 1.5 g
Cholesterol: 1 mg
Vitamins: B3, C
Minerals: Potassium, Calcium

2 tbsp olive oil
2 garlic cloves, finely chopped
225 g/8 oz mushrooms, chopped
6 tbsp *Greek-style Yogurt* (see page 124)
salt and pepper
2 tbsp chopped parsley, to garnish

Heat the oil in a frying pan over a moderate heat and sauté the garlic for 30 seconds, stirring. Add the mushrooms and stir-fry for 5 minutes. Add the yogurt and seasoning and warm through.

Pour over the cooked and drained pasta and garnish with the parsley.

WALNUT SAUCE
—————— Italy ——————

Calories per serving: 293
Saturated fat: Medium
Protein: Medium
Carbohydrate: Low
Fibre: 2.25 g
Cholesterol: 6 mg
Vitamins: E, B group
Minerals: Calcium, Iron, Potassium

300 ml/¹/₂ pt *Greek-style Yogurt* (see page 124)
1 tsp yeast extract
175 g/6 oz shelled walnuts, finely chopped
salt and black pepper
4 tbsp grated Parmesan cheese, to serve
2 tbsp chopped parsley, to garnish

Mix the yogurt with the yeast extract and heat gently in a small saucepan. Stir in the nuts and seasoning.

Pour over the cooked and drained pasta and sprinkle over the cheese and some black pepper. Garnish with the parsley.

LENTIL SAUCE
———— *Italy* ————

Calories per serving: 265
Saturated fat: Low
Protein: High
Carbohydrate: High
Fibre: 9.5 g
Cholesterol: Nil
Vitamins: C, Beta-carotene
Minerals: Iron

1 tbsp olive oil
1 onion, finely chopped
1 garlic clove, finely chopped
1 leek, sliced
275 g/10 oz green or brown lentils
1 large carrot, cut into 4
1 bay leaf
800 ml/28 fl oz light vegetable
    stock or water
salt and black pepper

Heat the oil in a heavy-based saucepan over a moderate heat and sauté the onion until soft and transparent. Add the garlic and stir. Add the leeks and cook for 2 minutes more, stirring. Add the lentils, carrot, bay leaf and stock and simmer for 1 hour, or until the lentils are tender, adding extra liquid if necessary. Remove the carrot and bay leaf.

Purée two-thirds of the lentils in a blender and return to the remaining contents of the pan, stir. Check the seasoning, and add salt if necessary.

RED PEPPER AND CHILLI SAUCE
———— *Spain* ————

This piquant sauce goes well with pasta, but is also excellent with grilled fish.

Calories per serving: 50
Saturated fat: Low
Protein: Medium
Carbohydrate: High
Fibre: 1 g
Cholesterol: 1 mg
Vitamins: Beta-carotene, C
Minerals: Potassium

2 fresh chilli peppers
2 large red peppers, deseeded and
    chopped
1 dsp sugar
2 tbsp vinegar
6 canned anchovy fillets, drained

Slit the chillies and deseed them. Chop them as finely as you can, then put them in a blender with the rest of the ingredients and purée until it has the consistency of a smooth sauce. Serve gently warmed or cold.

PESTO
———— *Italy* ————

Pesto is very rich. Once made it will keep in the refrigerator for a week or two.

Calories per serving: 270
Saturated fat: Medium
Protein: Medium
Carbohydrate: Low
Fibre: 0.5 g
Cholesterol: 9 mg
Vitamins: E, C
Minerals: Calcium

1 large garlic clove
2 cups of chopped fresh basil leaves
2 tbsp pine nuts
50 g/2 oz grated Parmesan cheese
6 tbsp olive oil
salt and black pepper

Using a pestle and mortar, crush the garlic. Add the basil and pound to a paste with a little salt. Add the pine nuts and pound again, then repeat with the cheese.

Dribble in the oil, a little at a time, and continue pounding until you have a thick sauce. Add salt and pepper to taste.

Pesto goes well with all kinds of pasta and is nice stirred into minestrone. You can warm it gently to serve it, but do not bring it to the boil.

PASTA AND GRAINS

OLIVE OIL AND GARLIC SAUCE
Spain

This is a less rich version of the French aïoli, which includes eggs.

Calories for the total batch: 1570 (serves 4–10 people)
Saturated fat: Medium
Protein: Trace
Carbohydrate: Trace
Fibre: 1 g
Cholesterol: Nil
Vitamins: Trace
Minerals: Trace

8 plump garlic cloves
1 tsp salt
175 ml/6 fl oz extra-virgin olive oil

Using a pestle and mortar, pound the garlic and salt until well blended. Add the oil drop by drop and continue pounding until it has a smooth consistency.

This sauce is good with all grilled foods and can be used as a dip with crusty bread.

TOMATO SAUCE
Italy

Always have a batch of tomato sauce made up to hand, as it can be used in so many ways.

Calories per serving: 87
Saturated fat: Medium
Protein: Low
Carbohydrate: Low
Fibre: 1.5 g
Cholesterol: Nil
Vitamins: C, Beta-carotene
Minerals: Potassium

2 tbsp olive oil
1 onion, very finely chopped
1 garlic clove, chopped
425 g/15 oz canned tomatoes *or*
    425 g/15 oz ripe fresh tomatoes, skinned
1 dsp chopped parsley
1/2 tsp sugar
1 tbsp tomato paste
1 tsp lemon juice
1 bay leaf
1 dsp chopped basil
salt and black pepper
a little tomato juice, as necessary

Heat the oil in a frying pan over a moderate heat and sauté the onion until very soft – this may take 20 minutes or more. Add the garlic and stir. Add the remaining ingredients except the basil and tomato juice and simmer for 20–30 minutes until it becomes a rich sauce.

Remove the bay leaf and add the basil. Stir and season to taste. If the sauce has become too thick you can thin it with a little tomato juice.

I prefer the sauce made with canned tomatoes, unless the fresh tomatoes are really ripe and tasty.

Variations: add 1 teaspoon of Tabasco or chilli powder to taste for a spicier sauce (this adds no calories); add 50 g/ 2 oz chopped mushrooms for the last 5 minutes of cooking (adds 2 calories per portion); add one small chopped red pepper with the tomatoes (adds 4 calories per portion).

OPPOSITE: Red Pepper and Chilli Sauce (page 99); Pesto (page 99); rigatoni with Ricotta and Aubergine Sauce (page 98)

101

SALADS AND VEGETABLES

No Mediterranean cook would feel happy without a regular supply of seasonal salad stuffs and vegetables. In this chapter you will learn how to create tempting main-course salads and vegetable and salad side dishes from the widest possible array of health-giving produce.

No traveller to any of the countries of the Mediterranean can fail to be impressed by the glorious fruit and vegetable markets with their piles of huge, plump ripe beef tomatoes, glossy aubergines, colourful peppers, giant melons, firm sun-ripened Spanish onions and the long plaits of Provence garlic...

With such colourful variety, the Mediterraneans have become experts at creating unusual combinations of salads, vegetables, fruits and nuts, sometimes with cheeses or small amounts of fish or meat.

The main-course salad recipes in this section are partly traditional, like the classic Salade Niçoise from France, and partly created by me using typical Mediterranean ingredients readily available over here. Most of these dishes also make good starters, serving about 8 people.

My side salads are ideal accompaniments to plain grilled meat, fish or cheese, and may also be eaten as light starters. Some Mediterranean side salads are so simple that they need no recipe: sliced cucumber with lemon juice and black pepper is wonderful with an oily fish dish; a plate of thickly sliced ripe tomatoes coated with oil is marvellous with grilled chicken; cold skinned and sliced grilled red peppers or cold cooked broad beans and finely chopped parsley are delicious served with roast or grilled pork and lamb.

Plainly cooked vegetables are usually the best garnish for main-course dishes. They may be steamed, baked, braised, lightly boiled in a little water, or roasted, and perhaps topped with some fresh chopped herbs such as chives, mint or marjoram. However, if you are serving a plain fish, poultry or meat dish, then it is appropriate to serve a slightly more elaborate vegetable dish. Some of the vegetable recipes here are substantial enough to make satisfying supper dishes on their own, perhaps with the addition of a little grated Parmesan cheese or a chunk of crusty bread.

OPPOSITE: Salade Niçoise (page 106)

MAIN COURSE SALADS

BROAD BEAN AND PASTA SALAD IN ORANGE SAUCE
Italy

Calories per serving: 227
Saturated fat: Low
Protein: Medium
Carbohydrate: High
Fibre: 6 g
Cholesterol: 1 mg
Vitamins: C, Niacin, Folic acid
Minerals: Iron, Potassium,
Calcium

140 g/5 oz (dry weight) pasta shells
175 g/6 oz tender young broad
  beans, lightly boiled
110 g/4 oz red kidney beans,
  canned, drained
50 g/2 oz button mushrooms, sliced
140 ml/¼ pt *Greek-style Yogurt* (see
  page 124)
1 orange
1 tbsp chopped parsley
8 whole lettuce leaves
1 tbsp chopped walnuts
salt and black pepper

Boil the pasta shells in salted water until just *al dente* and leave to cool slightly, then mix with the beans and mushrooms.

Blend the yogurt with the juice of half the orange, seasoning and parsley. Peel and chop the remaining orange and add to salad.

Arrange the lettuce in a serving bowl; pile the salad into the centre and pour over the dressing, tossing lightly. Scatter the walnuts over the top.

PASTA CRUNCH
Italy

Calories per serving: 390
Saturated fat: Low
Protein: Medium
Carbohydrate: Medium
Fibre: 5 g
Cholesterol: 30 mg
Vitamins: Beta-carotene, C, E,
Niacin, Folic acid
Minerals: Iron, Potassium,
Calcium

175 g/6 oz (dry weight) penne or
  pasta spirals
1 garlic clove, crushed
4 tbsp *Oil and Vinegar Dressing* (see
  page 110)
175 g/6 oz skinned cooked chicken,
  chopped into small pieces
1 large green pepper, deseeded and
  chopped
175 g/6 oz broccoli florets, very
  lightly boiled
1 red dessert apple, cored and
  chopped
3 tbsp sultanas
2 tbsp pine nuts

Boil the pasta in lightly salted water until just *al dente* and leave to cool slightly.

Stir the garlic into the dressing.
Combine all the ingredients and serve.

LENTIL AND TOMATO SALAD
—————— *Italy* ——————

Calories per serving: 358
Saturated fat: Low
Protein: Medium
Carbohydrate: Low
Fibre: 8 g
Cholesterol: 62 mg
Vitamins: C, Beta-carotene, D, E
Minerals: Iron, Potassium

225 g/8 oz green or brown lentils
1 small onion, halved
1 bay leaf
1 large beef tomato, chopped
8 spring onions, chopped
6 tbsp *Oil and Vinegar Dressing* (see page 110)
1 hard-boiled egg, chopped
2 tbsp chopped parsley

Cover the lentils with water in a saucepan and boil with the small onion and bay leaf until tender – about 1 hour. Drain them, remove the onion and bay leaf and leave them to cool slightly.

In a serving dish, combine the lentils with the tomato, spring onions and dressing. Sprinkle over the egg and parsley.

AVOCADO WITH LAMB'S LETTUCE
—————— *France* ——————

Calories per serving: 253
Saturated fat: Medium
Protein: Low
Carbohydrate: Low
Fibre: 3.5 g
Cholesterol: Nil
Vitamins: Beta-carotene, C, Folic acid
Minerals: Potassium, Iron

2 ripe avocados
140 g/5 oz lamb's lettuce leaves
8 sprigs of watercress
1 large beef tomato, deseeded and sliced
1 small onion, finely chopped
12 basil leaves, chopped
for the dressing:
2 tbsp olive oil
1 tbsp lemon juice
1 level tsp Dijon mustard
1/2 level tsp sugar
salt and black pepper

Combine the dressing ingredients thoroughly in a small bowl.

Peel, halve, stone and slice the avocados into a bowl and pour over the dressing to prevent them from discolouring.

Arrange the lettuce, watercress, tomato and onion in a serving bowl and add the avocado, pouring the remaining dressing over. Garnish with basil leaves.

SEAFOOD SALAD WITH THREE-JUICE DRESSING
—————— *Spain* ——————

Calories per serving: 238
Saturated fat: Low
Protein: High
Carbohydrate: Low
Fibre: 0.5 g
Cholesterol: 100 mg
Vitamins: C, Beta-carotene
Minerals: Iron, Calcium

1 large glass of white wine
juice of 1/2 lemon
225 g/8 oz prepared squid, sliced
8 frisée leaves
325 g/12 oz jar mussels in brine, gently rinsed and drained
5 cm/2 in piece of cucumber, chopped
1 small red pepper, deseeded and cut into squares
1 tbsp chopped parsley
for the dressing:
3 tbsp olive oil
1 tbsp each orange, lemon and lime juice
salt and black pepper

Put the wine and lemon juice in a small pan with a cup of water and bring to the boil. Add the squid and simmer gently for 5 minutes, then drain immediately.

Arrange the frisée leaves on a serving plate. Combine the dressing ingredients well. Mix the rest of ingredients with the dressing and pile this on the frisée leaves.

Garnish with orange, lime and lemon slices if wished.

SALAD NIÇOISE
———— *France* ————

Some versions of salade Niçoise add cooked potatoes, but I prefer to omit them and instead serve the salad with some crusty French bread.

Calories per serving: 328
Saturated fat: Medium
Protein: High
Carbohydrate: Low
Fibre: 3 g
Cholesterol: 291 mg
Vitamins: C, Beta-carotene, E, D, A
Minerals: Iron, Potassium

1 soft round lettuce
1 large beef tomato, chopped
75 g/3 oz cooked French beans
6 spring onions, halved
1 garlic clove, crushed
4 tbsp *Oil and Vinegar Dressing* (see page 110)
400 g/14 oz canned tuna in oil, drained
6 canned anchovy fillets, drained
8 stoned black olives
4 hard-boiled eggs

Remove the outer leaves of the lettuce and tear them into 2 or 3 pieces. Quarter the lettuce heart.

In a serving bowl, combine the torn lettuce and lettuce quarters with the tomato, beans and spring onions. Mix the garlic into the dressing and pour half of it over the contents of the bowl. Add the tuna in large chunks and place the anchovy fillets and olives on top.

Pour over the rest of the dressing. Quarter the eggs and arrange them on the top of the salad to serve.

PRAWN SALAD
———— *Spain* ————

The success of this dish depends upon the avocados being creamy-soft – almost on the point of being over-ripe.

Calories per serving: 526
Saturated fat: Low
Protein: Medium
Carbohydrate: Low
Fibre: 3.5 g
Cholesterol: 162 mg
Vitamins: C, Beta-carotene, E, Folic acid
Minerals: Potassium, Calcium

225 g/8 oz long-grain rice
1 sachet of saffron
1 large or 2 small ripe avocados
1 tbsp lemon juice
325 g/12 oz peeled cooked prawns
6 spring onions, chopped
1 small green pepper, deseeded and chopped
1 small red pepper, deseeded and chopped
4 tbsp *Oil and Vinegar Dressing* (see page 110)

Cook the rice with the saffron in lightly salted water until tender.

Meanwhile, peel, stone and slice the avocado into a bowl with the lemon juice, making sure it is well covered with the juice to prevent discoloration.

When the rice is cooked and still warm, combine it in a serving bowl with the rest of the ingredients.

This dish looks good garnished with a few prawns in their shells. Chopped dill can also be added as a garnish.

OPPOSITE: Prawn Salad

THREE-NUT SALAD WITH APRICOTS AND RAISINS

Italy

This sophisticated salad can also serve 8 as a dinner-party starter.

Calories per serving: 306
Saturated fat: Low
Protein: Low
Carbohydrate: Low
Fibre: 7 g
Cholesterol: Nil
Vitamins: E, Beta-carotene, C
Minerals: Iron, Calcium, Potassium

1 small head of radicchio
1 head of chicory
1 bunch of watercress, stalks removed
50 g/2 oz shelled walnuts, quartered
50 g/2 oz whole almonds
25 g/1 oz pine nuts
2 tbsp raisins
2 tbsp chopped dried apricots
1 celery stalk, chopped
for the dressing:
2 tbsp walnut or safflower oil
2 tbsp lemon juice
$\frac{1}{2}$ tsp runny honey
salt and black pepper

Tear each of the radicchio leaves into 2 or 3 pieces and put them in a serving bowl. Slice the chicory into rounds about 2.5 cm/1 in thick and break a few of them up. Add the rest of ingredients.

Combine the dressing ingredients thoroughly and pour over the salad. Toss well.

MIXED MEDITERRANEAN PLATTER

Italy

The essence of this salad is the variety of lovely colours on one large plate.

Calories per serving: 322
Saturated fat: Medium
Protein: Medium
Carbohydrate: Low
Fibre: 11 g
Cholesterol: 14 mg
Vitamins: Beta-carotene, C, E, Folic acid, Niacin
Minerals: Iron, Calcium

8 radicchio leaves
8 young spinach leaves
110 g/4 oz canned cannellini beans, rinsed and drained
3 tbsp *Oil and Vinegar Dressing* (see page 110)
a few basil leaves, chopped
5 cm/2 in piece of cucumber, thinly sliced
12 baby sweetcorn, lightly boiled
2 canned red peppers, drained and sliced
8 stoned black olives
1 beef tomato, cut into 8 slices
100 g/3$\frac{1}{2}$ oz Mozzarella cheese, cut into 8 slices
8 small round slices of wholemeal bread, about 7.5 cm/3 in diameter, toasted

On a large oval serving platter, arrange the radicchio on one half and the spinach on the other. Toss the beans in 1 tablespoon of the dressing, place them on the radicchio and garnish with some of the basil.

Arrange the cucumber next to the beans. Place the sweetcorn on the spinach and drizzle over a little dressing. Combine the red pepper slices with a little more basil and the olives and arrange this on the spinach.

Place a slice of tomato and then a slice of cheese on each of the bread rounds and grill until the cheese begins to bubble. Don't overcook or the cheese will be leathery.

Arrange the toast in the centre of the platter and drizzle any remaining dressing over the dish.

SIDE SALADS

TOMATO SALAD
——— France ———

Calories per serving: 46
Saturated fat: Low
Protein: Low
Carbohydrate: Low
Fibre: 1.5 g
Cholesterol: Nil
Vitamins: Beta-carotene, C, E
Minerals: Potassium

2 large beef tomatoes, sliced
1 tbsp olive oil
sea salt and black pepper
1 garlic clove, chopped
a few basil leaves, chopped

Arrange the tomato slices on 4 plates. Drizzle over the olive oil; sprinkle on a little salt and plenty of black pepper and sprinkle with the garlic and basil.

CARROT, APPLE AND BEET SALAD
——— Spain ———

Calories per serving: 97
Saturated fat: Low
Protein: Low
Carbohydrate: Low
Fibre: 2.5 g
Cholesterol: Nil
Vitamins: Beta-carotene, C,
  Folic acid
Minerals: Potassium

2 carrots, grated
1 cooked beetroot, weighing about
  110 g/4 oz, grated
2 tbsp raisins
2 tbsp *Oil and Vinegar Dressing* (see
  page 110)
1 dessert apple

Combine the carrot, beet, raisins and dressing in a serving bowl. Chop the unpeeled apple very finely and add it to the salad.

CELERY AND ARTICHOKE SALAD
——— Italy ———

I find canned artichoke hearts perfectly acceptable in this dish.

Calories per serving: 108
Saturated fat: Low
Protein: Low
Carbohydrate: Low
Fibre: 3 g
Cholesterol: Nil
Vitamins: Beta-carotene, C
Minerals: Calcium, Potassium

1 small head of celery, cut into
  7.5 cm/3 in strips
400 g/14 oz canned artichoke
  hearts, thoroughly drained and
  cut into halves
8 stoned black olives, chopped
a few celery leaves
3 tbsp *Oil and Vinegar Dressing* (see
  page 110)
1 tsp celery seeds

Arrange the celery and artichoke hearts on serving plates. Divide the olives between the plates.
  Pour some dressing on each plate and garnish with the celery leaves and seeds.

OIL AND VINEGAR DRESSING
—————— *France* ——————

Makes 14 tablespoons
Calories per tbsp: 98
Saturated fat: Low
Protein: Low
Carbohydrate: Low
Fibre: Nil
Cholesterol: Nil
Vitamins: Trace
Minerals: Trace

175 ml/6 fl oz extra-virgin olive oil
3 tbsp red wine vinegar
1 level tsp mustard powder
1 level tsp sugar
salt and plenty of black pepper

Combine all the ingredients in a screw-top jar. The dressing will keep for weeks in the refrigerator.

Variations: add chopped fresh herbs, such as tarragon, oregano or thyme; add crushed garlic; use white wine vinegar instead of red.

GREEN SALAD
—————— *France* ——————

Calories per serving: 56
Saturated fat: Low
Protein: Low
Carbohydrate: Low
Fibre: 1 g
Cholesterol: Nil
Vitamins: Beta-carotene, C, E
Minerals: Iron, Calcium

½ cos lettuce
8 frisée leaves
1 bunch of watercress
8 dandelion leaves
2 tbsp *Oil and Vinegar Dressing* (see above)
chopped chives, to garnish

Make sure all the leaves are clean but don't soak them in water. Tear the cos leaves and the frisée and chop off most of the watercress stalks. Combine all the leaves in a serving bowl with the dressing. Garnish with a few chopped chives.

Variation: for a fresher taste, add a little chicory and/or rocket and radicchio; if you can't find dandelion leaves, use lamb's lettuce, oak leaves or soft round lettuce leaves; for a milder taste, use iceberg lettuce instead of cos; add some chopped fresh herbs of your choice, such as chervil, basil, parsley or coriander.

POTATO SALAD
—————— *France* ——————

Potatoes in salads are often dressed in mayonnaise, but I am sure you will find this version superior.

Calories per serving: 190
Saturated fat: Low
Protein: Low
Carbohydrate: Medium
Fibre: 1.5 g
Cholesterol: Nil
Vitamins: C
Minerals: Potassium

450 g/1 lb new potatoes, scrubbed
4 tbsp *Oil and Vinegar Dressing* (see above)
2 tbsp chopped mint
2 tbsp chopped parsley
4 large spring onions, chopped

Boil the potatoes in salted water until just tender and then roughly chop them into a serving bowl. While the potatoes are still warm, add all the other ingredients and mix lightly. Cover and leave to stand for 1 hour before serving.

OPPOSITE: Green Salad with Oil and Vinegar Dressing; Potato Salad

TABBOULEH
—— *Lebanon* ——

Tabbouleh can be served as a starter. It also goes well with grilled lamb and fish.

Calories per serving: 170
Saturated fat: Low
Protein: Low
Carbohydrate: Medium
Fibre: 4 g
Cholesterol: Nil
Vitamins: Beta-carotene, C, E
Minerals: Calcium, Iron, Potassium

110 g/4 oz bulgar (cracked wheat)
1 cos lettuce
1 large beef tomato, deseeded and chopped
8 spring onions, chopped
7.5 cm/3 in piece of cucumber, chopped
1 bunch of mint, chopped
1 bunch of parsley, chopped
2 tbsp olive oil
2 tbsp lemon juice
salt and black pepper

Cover the bulgar with water and let it swell for 20 minutes. Drain well. Arrange the lettuce leaves around the edge of 4 serving dishes. Combine all the remaining ingredients and pile them on the serving dishes.

ORANGE AND FENNEL SALAD
—— *Italy* ——

This salad goes particularly well with oily fish and pork.

Calories per serving: 160
Saturated fat: Low
Protein: Low
Carbohydrate: Low
Fibre: 5 g
Cholesterol: Nil
Vitamins: C, Niacin, Beta-carotene
Minerals: Potassium, Calcium, Iron

1 large or 2 small fennel bulbs
2 large or 3 small oranges
4 tbsp olive oil
1 tbsp lemon juice
4 tbsp chopped parsley or coriander leaves
a few anise seeds
salt and black pepper

Wash, core and slice the fennel, keeping a few leaves to decorate the salad. Segment or thinly slice the oranges and arrange them on serving plates with the fennel in the centre.

Blend the olive oil, lemon juice and seasoning and dribble this over the salads. Sprinkle the parsley or coriander and anise seeds on top and decorate with fennel leaves.

BEAN SALAD
—— *Italy* ——

Calories per serving: 192
Saturated fat: Low
Protein: Medium
Carbohydrate: Low
Fibre: 11 g
Cholesterol: Nil
Vitamins: C
Minerals: Potassium, Calcium

175 g/6 oz dried haricot beans, soaked in water overnight
1 bay leaf
3 tbsp *Oil and Vinegar Dressing* (see page 110)
1 garlic clove, crushed
2 celery stalks, chopped
4 spring onions, chopped
1 tbsp chopped parsley

Drain the beans. Put them in a saucepan with water to cover and boil for 10 minutes, then turn the heat down, add the bay leaf and simmer gently until tender – up to 2 hours. Drain and mix with the rest of the ingredients while still warm.

Flageolet beans also work well in this dish.

OPPOSITE: Orange and Fennel Salad; Tabbouleh

VEGETABLES

PURÉED PUMPKIN
──────── *France* ────────

Calories per serving: 100
Saturated fat: Low
Protein: Low
Carbohydrate: Low
Fibre: 1.5 g
Cholesterol: Nil
Vitamins: Beta-carotene, C
Minerals: Potassium

675 g/1½ lb pumpkin (squash), peeled, deseeded and cubed
pinch of sugar
2 garlic cloves, chopped
1½ tbsp olive oil
salt
1 tsp paprika
1 dsp toasted sesame seeds

Preheat the oven to 180°C/350°F/gas 4.

In a shallow ovenproof dish mix the pumkin with the rest of the ingredients except the seeds. Cover and bake for 30 minutes to 1 hour, until tender.

Eat as soon as it comes out of the oven, or purée it in a blender. Sprinkle the sesame seeds over before serving.

Variation: you can use this recipe for sweet potatoes, but the calorie count goes up to 205.

PURÉED POTATOES
──────── *France* ────────

Most people add butter to puréed potatoes, but this recipe is a healthier alternative.

Calories per serving: 197
Saturated fat: Low
Protein: Low
Carbohydrate: High
Fibre: 2 g
Cholesterol: Nil
Vitamins: C
Minerals: Potassium

675 g/1½ lb floury potatoes
2 tbsp olive oil
2 tbsp *Greek-style Yogurt* (see page 124)
salt and pepper

Boil the potatoes in their skins. Peel them and chop them into a bowl or blender. Add the olive oil, salt and pepper and blend to a purée. Fold in the yogurt just before serving.

RATATOUILLE
──────── *France* ────────

Some versions of ratatouille contain little aubergine, but I prefer it to be dominant.

Calories per serving: 143
Saturated fat: Low
Protein: Low
Carbohydrate: Low
Fibre: 5.5 g
Cholesterol: Nil
Vitamins: Beta-carotene, C, E
Minerals: Potassium, Iron

1 large aubergine
2 courgettes
3 tbsp olive oil
1 large onion, sliced
1 large garlic clove, chopped
1 green pepper, deseeded and sliced
200 g/7 oz canned tomatoes
1 dsp chopped fresh basil or 1 tsp dried
salt and black pepper

Slice the aubergines and courgettes, sprinkle them with salt and leave them in a colander to drain for 30 minutes. Rinse and pat dry.

Heat the oil in a flameproof casserole over a moderate heat and sauté the onion until soft. Add the garlic and sauté for another minute. Add the aubergine, courgette, pepper and seasoning. Cover and simmer for 40 minutes. Then add the tomatoes and basil and simmer, uncovered, for 20 minutes.

SPINACH WITH GARLIC AND OIL
—— *Italy* ——

Calories per serving: 95
Saturated fat: Low
Protein: High
Carbohydrate: Low
Fibre: 10 g
Cholesterol: Nil
Vitamins: Beta-carotene, C, E
Minerals: Potassium, Calcium

675 g/1½ lb fresh spinach, rinsed
   and chopped
1 tbsp olive oil
1 garlic clove, chopped
pinch of grated nutmeg
2 tbsp grated Parmesan cheese
salt and black pepper

Cook the spinach in the water clinging to its leaves in a covered saucepan until wilted. Drain.

Heat the oil in frying pan over a moderate heat and stir-fry the spinach with the garlic and nutmeg for a minute or two. Season to taste, transfer to a serving dish and top with the cheese.

SWISS CHARD WITH PINE NUTS
—— *Italy* ——

Calories per serving: 80
Saturated fat: Low
Protein: High
Carbohydrate: Low
Fibre: 6.5 g
Cholesterol: Nil
Vitamins: Beta-carotene, C, E
Minerals: Iron, Calcium

450 g/1 lb chard leaves, trimmed
1 tbsp olive oil
2 tbsp pine nuts
2 garlic cloves, chopped
pinch of grated nutmeg
salt and black pepper

Parboil the chard for a few minutes.

Heat the oil in a frying pan over a moderate heat and sauté the pine nuts until golden. Remove with a slotted spoon,. Sauté the chard for 2 minutes, adding the garlic for the last minute.

Season with nutmeg, salt and pepper. Serve with the pine nuts scattered over.

FRENCH BEANS IN ORANGE SAUCE
—— *France* ——

Calories per serving: 75
Saturated fat: Low
Protein: Low
Carbohydrate: Low
Fibre: 3.5 g
Cholesterol: Nil
Vitamins: C, E
Minerals: Potassium

450 g/1 lb tender young French
   beans
1 tbsp olive oil
2 spring onions, finely chopped
1 tsp Dijon mustard
1 tbsp orange juice
dash of white wine vinegar

Top and tail the beans and parboil them in lightly salted water for 2 minutes.

Heat the oil in a frying pan over a moderate heat, add the onions and stir-fry them for 1 minute. Add the mustard, orange juice and vinegar and stir-fry for another minute. Add the beans and stir-fry for another minute and serve.

PEPPER AND TOMATO STEW
—— *Spain* ——

Calories per serving: 66
Saturated fat: Low
Protein: Low
Carbohydrate: Low
Fibre: 3 g
Cholesterol: Nil
Vitamins: Beta-carotene, C, E
Minerals: Potassium

1 tbsp olive oil
1 onion, thinly sliced
1 garlic clove, chopped
1 green pepper, seeded and sliced
2 beef tomatoes, sliced
1 level tsp ground coriander
1 level tsp ground cumin
salt and black pepper

Heat the oil in a heavy-based saucepan over a moderate heat and sauté the onion until soft. Add the garlic and pepper and sauté for 1 minute. Add the rest of ingredients, bring to a simmer, cover and cook for 30 minutes.

Variation: omit the spices and add 2 teaspoons of chopped basil.

OVERLEAF: Puréed Pumpkin; Swiss Chard with Pine Nuts

BREAKFASTS
AND DESSERTS

Even a diet of the healthiest lunches and suppers can be sabotaged if you continue to indulge in fatty cooked breakfasts and sugary desserts.

Here instead are some light and healthy Mediterranean-style carbohydrate-rich breakfast choices and mouth-watering desserts based on fruit.

The Northern European passion for animal protein at breakfast time – slices of bacon, sausages, black pudding, eggs, ham, and so on – is virtually non-existent among the peoples of the Mediterranean region.

Breakfast in Spain, Italy, Greece and the South of France is much more of a high-carbohydrate affair. Carbohydrate is, in fact, a much more sensible breakfast, as it is more quickly converted by the body into much-needed energy to get you started for the day.

The perfect breakfast is plenty of fresh crusty bread with preserves or honey, some fresh fruit juice or fruit and – for the big breakfast eater – some Greek-style yogurt.

The yogurt of the Eastern Mediterranean is strained and beautifully thick and creamy. It may seem like a real indulgence until you discover that it does, in fact, contain only about half the fat of our ordinary single cream.

However, for calorie-watchers, I have devised an even lower-fat, lower-calorie version, which tastes almost as good as the real thing and is easy to make. If you prefer to buy real Greek yogurt, be aware that it contains 20 calories per tablespoon rather than the 10 in my version. Ordinary low-fat natural yogurt can also be used in most of the recipes and at breakfast; some brands taste creamier and richer than others.

Desserts in the Mediterranean were traditionally fairly simple and usually based on fruit. It is only recently in the more affluent areas, and with the increase in tourism, that desserts in restaurants in the area have become elaborate, more fat-laden and less healthy.

I would almost always choose to end any Mediterranean meal with fresh fruit, but I have included a few more elaborate dessert recipes as everyone enjoys an indulgence now and then – and I am no exception in this!

OPPOSITE: Peaches in Wine (page 120)

MIXED FRUIT COMPOTE
———— Tunisia ————

Calories per serving: 260
Saturated fat: Nil
Protein: Low
Carbohydrate: High
Fibre: 18 g
Cholesterol: Nil
Vitamins: A, C, Beta-carotene
Minerals: Iron, Potassium

175 g/6 oz dried apricots or peaches
110 g/3½ oz stoned prunes
450 ml/¾ pt orange juice
2 oranges
2 bananas
50 g/2 oz raisins

In an ovenproof dish soak the apricots and prunes overnight in the orange juice.

Preheat the oven to 180°C/350°F/gas 4.

Peel and slice the oranges and bananas into rounds and add them and the raisins to the dish. Bake for 30 minutes and serve hot or cold.

Variations: you can vary the fruit according to what is available; try figs or dates instead of prunes.

PEACHES IN WINE
———— France ————

Calories per serving: 115
Saturated fat: Nil
Protein: Low
Carbohydrate: High
Fibre: 1.5 g
Cholesterol: Nil
Vitamins: C, Beta-carotene
Minerals: Potassium

4 ripe peaches
25 g/1 oz caster sugar
juice of ½ lemon
about 200 ml/7 fl oz dessert wine,
    such as a Muscat

Skin the peaches and slice them into serving dishes. Sprinkle with the sugar and lemon juice.

Before serving, pour over enough wine just to cover the peaches.

CITRUS AND HONEY DESSERT
———— Italy ————

Calories per serving: 140
Saturated fat: Low
Protein: Low
Carbohydrate: Medium
Fibre: 3 g
Cholesterol: Nil
Vitamins: C, E, Beta-carotene
Minerals: Potassium

2 oranges
2 ruby grapefruit
juice of ½ lemon
3 tbsp orange juice
2 tbsp runny honey
2 tbsp chopped mixed nuts, to
    garnish

Peel and segment the oranges and grapefruit and arrange them in serving bowls.

Stir together the juices and honey and heat gently in a small pan, or in the microwave. Pour over the fruit, and garnish with the chopped nuts.

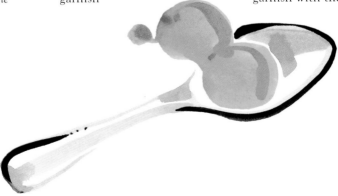

APPLE AND DATE COMPOTE
—— Greece ——

Calories per serving: 155
Saturated fat: Low
Protein: Low
Carbohydrate: High
Fibre: 6 g
Cholesterol: Nil
Vitamins: C, Folic acid
Minerals: Potassium

4 large cooking apples
50 g/2 oz stoned dates, chopped
1/2 level tsp ground cinnamon
juice from 2 oranges
2 tbsp runny honey
2 tbsp sesame seeds

Preheat the oven to 190°C/375°F/gas 5.

Peel and slice the apples into a shallow ovenproof dish and mix in the dates with the cinnamon. Pour over the orange juice and honey and top with the sesame seeds. Bake for 30 minutes.

BANANA AND STRAWBERRY SORBETS
—— Italy ——

Calories per serving: 185
Saturated fat: Low
Protein: Low
Carbohydrate: High
Fibre: 3 g
Cholesterol: Trace
Vitamins: Beta-carotene, C
Minerals: Iron, Potassium

110 g/4 oz caster sugar
2 ripe bananas
2 tbsp lemon juice
175 ml/6 fl oz Greek-style Yogurt
  (see page 124)
225 g/8 oz ripe strawberries
strawberry leaves, to garnish

Dissolve the sugar in 200 ml/7 fl oz water and boil to make a syrup. Mash the bananas with half the lemon juice, the yogurt and half the syrup.

Purée the strawberries with the remaining lemon juice and syrup. Freeze both in different containers, removing from the freezer from time to time to whisk.

Serve a spoonful of each variety to each person, garnished with the strawberry leaves.

Variations: use raspberries instead of strawberries, or melon or mango instead of one of the bananas.

MELON AND STRAWBERRY SALAD
—— Italy ——

Calories per serving: 80
Saturated fat: Nil
Protein: Low
Carbohydrate: High
Fibre: 3.5 g
Cholesterol: Nil
Vitamins: Beta-carotene, C,
  Folic acid
Minerals: Iron

2 small ripe Ogen or Cantaloupe
  melons
325 g/12 oz ripe strawberries
1 tbsp lemon juice
1 level tbsp sugar
12 mint leaves

Halve the melons horizontally, remove and discard the seeds and scoop out and retain the flesh. Hull the strawberries and coarsely chop them. Cover with the lemon juice and sugar and leave for 30 minutes.

Mix the melon flesh and strawberries and pile this back into the melon skins. Decorate with the mint leaves.

OVERLEAF: Mixed Fruit Compote; Citrus and Honey
Dessert; Apple and Date Compote

BAKED PEARS
—————— France ——————

Calories per serving: 172
Saturated fat: Nil
Protein: Low
Carbohydrate: High
Fibre: 3 g
Cholesterol: Nil
Vitamins: C
Minerals: Potassium

4 firm pears, such as Conference
75 g/3 oz sugar
½ bottle of red wine
4 cloves
1 cinnamon stick

Preheat the oven to 160°C/325°F/ gas 3.

Peel the pears, leaving the stalks on. Place them in an ovenproof dish with the sugar and wine. Add the cinnamon stick and the cloves and water to cover.

Bake until the pears are tender. If the juice is too thin, reduce it in a saucepan. Pour it over the pears and serve cold.

Variations: pears can also be cooked this way in a covered saucepan over a very gentle heat.

GREEK-STYLE YOGURT
—————— Greece ——————

Calories per 140 ml/¼ pt serving: 67
Saturated fat: Low
Protein: High
Carbohydrate: Medium
Fibre: Nil
Cholesterol: 4.5 mg
Vitamins: Niacin, A
Minerals: Calcium

2 level tbsp skimmed milk powder
550 ml/18 fl oz skimmed milk
1 tbsp live Greek yogurt (as fresh as possible)

Dissolve the milk powder in the milk and simmer for 5 minutes. Pour into a heatproof bowl and allow to cool until you can just dip a finger in it. Add the yogurt and stir. Cover the bowl with film, wrap it in a thick towel and leave it in a warm place (an airing cupboard or a shelf above a cooker or radiator) for 5–6 hours. Alternatively, you can make the yogurt in a wide-necked vacuum flask.

When it is set, pour off the thin whey on top and pass the yogurt through a sieve lined with layers of kitchen paper, set over a bowl. Leave for 30 minutes by which time the yogurt will have thickened. Put in a covered container and chill in the refrigerator. Use a tablespoon of this yogurt to start your next batch.

The secret of making good yogurt lies in using a good fresh starter. Also keep all your utensils sterilized and do not leave the yogurt longer than necessary to set.

OPPOSITE: Greek-style Yogurt with fresh fruit

INDEX

126

INDEX

CONVERSION CHART

For most general purposes the term 'calorie' is used for the kilocalorie and this is the practice used throughout this book

Calories (kcal)	Kilojoules (kJ)	Calories (kcal)	Kilojoules (kJ)	Calories (kcal)	Kilojoules (kJ)	Calories (kcal)	Kilojoules (kJ)
1	4.18	400	1,670	1,300	5,435	2,000	8,360
50	210	500	2,090	1,400	5,850	2,100	8,780
100	420	600	2,510	1,500	6,270	2,250	9,405
150	630	750	3,135	1,600	6,690	2,500	10,450
200	835	1,000	4,180	1,700	7,105		
250	1,045	1,100	4,560	1,800	7,525		
300	1,255	1,200	5,015	1,900	7,940		

HEIGHT/WEIGHT CHART FOR WOMEN

Height	Average weight	Acceptable weight range
4 ft 11 in	104 lb	94–122 lb
1.50 m	47.25 k	42.75–55.5 k
5 ft 0 in	107 lb	96–125 lb
1.52.5 m	48.75 k	44–57 k
5 ft 1 in	110 lb	99–128 lb
1.55 m	50 k	45–58 k
5 ft 2 in	113 lb	102–131 lb
1.57.5 m	51.5 k	46.5–59.5 k
5 ft 3 in	116 lb	105–134 lb
1.60 m	52.75 k	47.75–61 k
5 ft 4 in	120 lb	108–138 lb
1.62.5 m	54.5 k	49–62.75 k
5 ft 5 in	123 lb	111–142 lb
1.65 m	56 k	50.5–64.5 k
5 ft 6 in	128 lb	114–146 lb
1.67.5 m	58 k	52–66 k
5 ft 7 in	132 lb	118–150 lb
1.70.5 m	60 k	54–68 k
5 ft 8 in	136 lb	122–154 lb
1.73 m	61 k	55.5–70 k
5 ft 9 in	140 lb	126–158 lb
1.75.5 m	63.5 k	57–72 k
5 ft 10 in	144 lb	130–163 lb
1.78 m	65.6	59–74 k
5 ft 11 in	148 lb	134–168 lb
1.80.5 m	67 k	61–76 k

HEIGHT/WEIGHT CHART FOR MEN

Height	Average weight	Acceptable weight range
5 ft 4 in	130 lb	118–148 lb
1.62.5 m	59 k	53.5–67 k
5 ft 5 in	133 lb	121–152 lb
1.65 m	60.5 k	55–69 k
5 ft 6 in	136 lb	124–156 lb
1.67.5 m	62 k	56.5–71 k
5 ft 7 in	140 lb	128–161 lb
1.70.5 m	63.5 k	58–73 k
5 ft 8 in	145 lb	132–166 lb
1.73 m	66 k	60–75.5 k
5 ft 9 in	149 lb	136–170 lb
1.75.5 m	68 k	62–77 k
5 ft 10 in	153 lb	140–174 lb
1.78 m	69.5 k	63.5–79 k
5 ft 11 in	158 lb	144–179 lb
1.80.5 m	72 k	65.5–81 k
6 ft 0 in	162 lb	148–184 lb
1.83 m	73.5 k	67–84 k
6 ft 1 in	166 lb	152–189 lb
1.85.5 m	75.5 kg	69–86 k
6 ft 2 in	171 lb	156–194 lb
1.88 m	78 k	71–88 k
6 ft 3 in	176 lb	160–199 lb
1.90.5 m	80 k	73–90 k
6 ft 4 in	181 lb	164–204 lb
1.93 m	82 k	75–93 k